Scandinavians in Michigan

Discovering the Peoples of Michigan is a series of publications examining the state's rich multicultural heritage. The series makes available an interesting, affordable, and varied collection of books that enables students and lay readers to explore Michigan's ethnic dynamics. A knowledge of the state's rapidly changing multicultural history has far-reaching implications for human relations, education, public policy, and planning. We believe that Discovering the Peoples of Michigan will enhance understanding of the unique contributions that diverse and often unrecognized communities have made to Michigan's history and culture.

Scandinavians in Michigan

Jeffrey W. Hancks

Michigan State University Press

East Lansing

⊗ The paper used in this publication meets the minimum requirements
of ANSI/NISO Z39.48-1992 (R 1997) (Permanence of Paper).

Michigan State University Press
East Lansing, Michigan 48823-5245

Printed and bound in the United States of America.
12 11 10 09 08 07 06   1 2 3 4 5 6 7 8 9 10

LIBRARY OF CONGRESS CATALOGING-IN-PUBLICATION DATA
Hancks, Jeffrey W.
Scandinavians in Michigan / Jeffrey W. Hancks.
p. cm.— (Discovering the peoples of Michigan)
Includes bibliographical references and index.
ISBN 0-87013-775-1 (pbk. : alk. paper) 1. Scandinavian Americans—Michigan—History.
2. Scandinavian Americans—Michigan—Social conditions. 3. Scandinavian Americans—
Michigan—Social life and customs. 4. Immigrants—Michigan—History. 5. Michigan—
Ethnic relations. 6. Michigan—Social conditions. 7. Michigan—Social life and customs.
I. Title. II. Series.
F575.S18H36 2006
977.40043'95—dc22
2006005183

Discovering the Peoples of Michigan. The editors wish to thank
the Kellogg Foundation for their generous support.

Cover design by Ariana Grabec-Dingman
Book design by Sharp Des!gns, Lansing, Michigan
Cover photo: Representatives of the Nordic countries participating in a 1970s ethnic
summer festival held along Detroit's riverfront, posed in front of their respective flags,
dressed in traditional costumes. (Courtesy of the Christian T. Feddersen Collection,
Michigan Historical Collections, Bentley Historical Library, University of Michigan.)

Visit Michigan State University Press on the World Wide Web at *www.msupress.msu.edu*

DEDICATION

This book is dedicated to many people in the United States and Denmark who have played an integral role in my personal and professional development.

To the outstanding faculty and graduate students at the University of Wisconsin-Madison Department of Scandinavian Studies for offering me the opportunity to deepen my knowledge of the Scandinavian countries and providing me with priceless teaching experience; especially Nete Schmidt, Niels Ingwersen, Susan Brantly, Tanya Thresher, Scott Mellor, and Katarina Tucker.

To my mentors and former colleagues at the Wisconsin Historical Society Library in Madison for allowing me the opportunity to gain invaluable experience as a public services librarian at a world-class institution; especially Laura Hemming, Nancy Mulhern, Jim Hansen, and Rick Pifer.

To my former colleagues and supervisors at the Clarke Historical Library and the Park Library at Central Michigan University for taking a chance on hiring a new librarian, modeling the practice of librarianship, and providing a stimulating, exciting work environment; especially Marian Matyn, Jennifer Wood, Mary Graham, Pat Thelen, Frank Boles, Michael Lorenzen, Stephanie Mathson, and Thomas Moore.

To my host families and friends in Denmark for opening your homes, minds, and hearts to a timid seventeen-year-old boy from small-town Illinois, and helping mold a citizen of the world. I cannot begin to express my eternal gratitude adequately in a few short words. Ten years has gone by quickly, and I look forward to many more years of your friendship; Kirsten and Henning Knudsen, Karin and Erik Svendsen, Finn Mikkelsen and Kaja Gissel, Jan Johannesen and Grethe Pedersen, the members of the Grenaa and Grenaa-Djurs Rotary Clubs, and most especially Jytte and Per Reng.

Above all, I dedicate this book to my parents, Murray and Vickie Hancks, and my brother Matt Hancks. Your love, wisdom, support, and courage to allow me to explore the world at such an early age forever shaped my view of humanity, and prepared me to bravely face whatever the future holds.

SERIES ACKNOWLEDGMENTS

Discovering the Peoples of Michigan is a series of publications that resulted from the cooperation and effort of many individuals. The people recognized here are not a complete representation, for the list of contributors is too numerous to mention. However, credit must be given to Jeffrey Bonevich, who worked tirelessly with me on contacting people as well as researching and organizing material.

The initial idea for this project came from Mary Erwin, but I must thank Fred Bohm, director of the Michigan State University Press, for seeing the need for this project, for giving it his strong support, and for making publication possible. Also, the tireless efforts of Keith Widder and Elizabeth Demers, senior editors at Michigan State University Press, were vital in bringing DPOM to fruition.

Otto Feinstein and Germaine Strobel of the Michigan Ethnic Heritage Studies Center patiently and willingly provided names for contributors and constantly gave this project their tireless support. Yvonne Lockwood of the Michigan State University Museum has also suggested and advised contributors.

Many of the maps in the series were prepared by Gregory Anderson at the Geographical Information Center (GIS) at Western Michigan University under the directorship of David Dickason. Additional maps have been contributed by Ellen White.

Other authors and organizations provided comments on other aspects of the work. There are many people that were interviewed by the various authors who will remain anonymous. However, they have enabled the story of their group to be told. Unfortunately, their names are not available, but we are grateful for their cooperation.

Most of all, this work is a tribute to the writers who patiently gave their time to write and share their research findings. Their contributions are noted and appreciated. To them goes most of the gratitude.

ARTHUR W. HELWEG, *Series Co-editor*

Contents

Introduction

The Scandinavian countries of Denmark, Norway, and Sweden are commonly grouped together because of the close historic, linguistic, and ethnic ties between the Danish, Norwegian, and Swedish peoples. Therefore, it is not unusual that the Danes, Norwegians, and Swedes, like the Germans and Swiss or the French and Walloons, are grouped together when discussing ethnic groups living in immigrant countries like the United States. While it is not always appropriate to group varying ethnicities together based solely upon historic, linguistic, or ethnic ties, there are significant reasons to link Scandinavian-Americans. The age-old bonds between the Scandinavian peoples continued to flourish both during and after the period of mass emigration from Scandinavia to the United States in the late nineteenth and early twentieth centuries. Scandinavians felt comfortable with each other, a feeling forged through centuries of familiarity, and they usually chose to live in close proximity to each other in communities throughout the Upper Midwest. The result was communities that developed and nurtured a distinct Scandinavian-American flavor. Numerous Scandinavian-American communities retain that essence today.

Many people include Iceland and Finland in addition to Denmark, Norway, and Sweden in their interpretations of Scandinavia. However, this interpretation is not entirely correct. Technically, Scandinavia refers to the geographic peninsula in northern Europe that Norway and Sweden share, but has come to include Denmark because of the close historic and cultural ties and mutually intelligible languages Danes, Norwegians, and Swedes share. While the Icelandic language belongs to the same Northern Germanic language family as Danish, Norwegian, and Swedish, and the island nation's inhabitants are descendents of Norwegian settlers, its extreme geographic isolation from the Scandinavian mainland has allowed the Icelandic language to remain virtually the same today as it was one thousand years ago, while the mainland languages have evolved greatly. Today, the languages are not mutually intelligible. The Finnish language, on the other hand, belongs to the Finno-Ugric language family and bears no similarity whatsoever to the Scandinavian languages. Finland's only linguistic tie to Scandinavia lies in the small, yet influential, Swedish-speaking minority living along Finland's southern and western coast. When including Finns and Icelanders, two nationalities who certainly share many of the same ideals and experiences with their Scandinavian brethren, the most correct collective term is Nordic. For the purposes of clarity, in this text Scandinavians are defined as Danes, Swedes, and Norwegians.

From the middle of the nineteenth century, until the 1920s, hundreds of thousands of Scandinavians decided to leave their homelands to make a new start for themselves in the United States and Canada. Within Scandinavia, Sweden had the greatest number of its citizens leave for the United States, with over one million migrating between 1820 and 1920. Per capita, Norway was the country most affected by the exodus, with over 850,000 Norwegians moving to America between 1820 and 1920. In fact, Norway ranks second only to Ireland in the percentage of its population that left for the New World. Denmark was affected to a much smaller extent, but it too lost over 300,000 of its citizens to the promise of America. Once made, the move was usually permanent, as few would ever return to live in Scandinavia again.

Michigan was never the most popular destination for Scandinavian immigrants. As immigrants began arriving in the North American interior, they settled in areas to the west of Michigan, particularly in Wisconsin, Minnesota, Illinois, Iowa, North Dakota, and South Dakota.

Native-Born Scandinavians in Michigan

	1850	1860	1870	1880	1890	1900
Danes	13	192	1,354	3,513	6,335	6,390
Norwegians	110	440	1,516	3,520	7,795	7,582
Swedes	16	266	2,406	9,412	27,366	26,956
Total Scandinavians	139	898	5,276	16,645	41,496	40,928
Total State Population	397,654	749,113	1,184,059	1,636,937	2,093,889	2,420,982
Percentage Scandinavians	0.03%	0.1%	0.4%	1.0%	1.98%	1.7%

Source: Nelson, O.N., *History of the Scandinavians and Successful Scandinavians in the United States* V. I and II, 2nd ed. (Minneapolis: O.N. Nelson, 1904), 256–60, 264a.

Nevertheless, thousands of Scandinavian immigrants decided to pursue their American dream in the Great Lakes State. They settled in Detroit and played an important role in the city's industrial boom and subsequent automotive industries. They settled in the Upper Peninsula and worked tirelessly in the abundant iron and copper mines. They settled in the northern Lower Peninsula and felled millions of trees. Finally, they settled in the fertile areas of West Michigan and contributed to the state's burgeoning agricultural sector. Today, their presence remains in town names like Amble in Montcalm County and Skandia in Marquette County and in local culinary delicacies like æbleskiver in Greenville and lutefisk found in select grocery stores throughout the state at Christmastime.

Denmark

Historical Context for Immigration

The southernmost and geographically smallest Scandinavian country, Denmark experienced a much lower rate of emigration than neighboring Norway and Sweden. This is due in large part to its relatively flat topography and fertile soil. Danish farmers were able to produce enough agricultural products to sustain themselves and their country-men. However, some Danes did decide to leave Europe for North America. The migration from Denmark to the United States was greatest between the years 1861 and 1930. The beginning of this period corresponds with the outbreak of the U.S. Civil War, during which many Danes supported the Union cause, and end of this period coincides with the implementation of the immigrant quota system during the Great Depression. During those seventy years, a total of 326,925 Danes migrated to the United States. The decade with the largest number of Danish immigrants was the 1880s, when 88,132 Danes left for America.[1] There were three primary reasons that the Danes left home. First, the promise of religious freedom, particularly for Mormons, attracted many Danes. Second, as with many Europeans, the Danes were tempted by the allure of cheap, abundant land in the United States. Third, many Danes living in the duchies of Schleswig and Holstein chose to emigrate to the United States after Denmark lost the Danish-Prussian war of 1864 and ceded the entire territory to German rule.

Mormon missionaries were particularly active in recruiting Danes to the faith. The Danish constitution of 1849 guaranteed the freedom of religion, so missionaries were free to practice in Denmark. Most Danes, while members of the state-sponsored Evangelical Lutheran church, were not particularly strong in their faith, and therefore were more receptive than other Europeans to the missionaries' message. The missionaries' efforts were relatively successful, and by 1905, 23,509 Danes had converted, with a majority of them coming from the rural province of Jutland.

Upon conversion, Danish Mormons were encouraged to leave Denmark for the United States. The very first wave of Danes to migrate to the United States consisted of newly converted Mormons. Between 1850 and 1870, 16,760 Danes left for the United States. Of that figure, 7,840 of them were Mormons. The missionaries' success in converting Danes to Mormonism increased greatly after the *Book of Mormon* was translated into Danish by the first Danish convert, Peter Clemmensen, following a personal appeal by church leader Brigham Young. Most Danish Mormon emigrants settled in the newly created Utah Territory, but before they set out for Utah, they met at staging areas located throughout Iowa. The Danes sailed for New York, continued by boat to Albany, New York, and then traveled by rail to Niagara and further to Windsor, Ontario. They crossed into Detroit and continued by rail to the staging areas. There is no evidence of any significant number of Danish Mormon converts settling permanently in Michigan.[2]

By the end of the nineteenth century, the ancient Danish practice of feudalism had long ceased to legally exist. However, its remnants still were in place, as many farmers were landless and forced to live and work on the farms of wealthy landowners. Additionally, the price of productive land was too high for most farmers to ever realistically wish to purchase their own farms. This was particularly a problem on the fertile southern Danish islands of Lolland and Falster. Further complicating matters, landowners on the islands took to raising sugar beets, which have a very short harvest season. Landless farmers could not earn enough money working during the short harvest to survive the

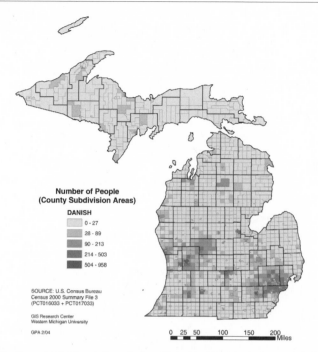

Distribution of Michigan's Population Claiming Danish Ancestry, U.S. Census 2000.

long winters. Lolland and Falster, in addition to inhospitably rocky and sandy areas like the island of Bornholm and northern and western Jutland, were the areas that provided the highest percentage of immigrants to North America. To the landless residents of these areas, the desire to own their own farms, particularly in the vast, empty American Midwest, was too tempting to resist.

The final major subgroup of Danes who chose to immigrate to North America was ethnic Danes living in the duchies of Schleswig and Holstein. For centuries, ethnic Danes and Germans lived side-by-side in the duchies, particularly in Schleswig. After a series of mid-nineteenth-century wars between the Danes and the Germanic peoples, however, Denmark was finally forced in 1864 to cede all of its claims to the two duchies, in addition to Lauenburg, to Austria-Prussia. The loss of the three duchies resulted in a reduction of almost 40 percent in Denmark's land area and population. Subsequent acts of forced

The Danish Sisterhood of America

Life for immigrants in America was not always glamorous. While thousands of Danes found their fortunes in the United States, many thousands more struggled to make a living. Illness, disease, hunger, and the inability to speak English served as a roadblock to success. By the 1870s, successful Danish immigrants began organizing themselves to provide for their less fortunate countrymen in the United States. The result of this organization was the creation of the Danish Brotherhood in America, a fraternal organization that sought to provide for the cultural and financial needs of Danish-born and Danish-American men. The success of the Danish Brotherhood of America spurred interest in creating a similar organization for Danish women. The push for a sister organization was led by Danish-born Negaunee, Michigan, resident Mrs. Christine Hemmingsen. On November 21, 1883, the Danish Sisterhood in America held an organizational meeting in Hemmingsen's Upper Peninsula home. The organization was formally chartered on December 1, 1883, and the Christine Lodge, with only five active members, was founded. To fill all of the posts needed to have a lodge, men were allowed to join as passive members. In subsequent years, lodges were created in cities throughout the upper Midwest and west and were often tied to a Danish Brotherhood lodge. In 1908, 106 lodges served 5,195 members, including 12 lodges and 533 members in Michigan.[1] Charitable deeds have long been a staple of the Sisterhood, and the sisters became particularly active in providing assistance to Denmark during the Second World War and in providing scholarships for students at Dana College in Nebraska.

Today fifty-six Danish Sisterhood in America lodges exist throughout the United States and Canada, with seven in Michigan, and nearly 2,000 active members. These include the original Christine Lodge 1 in Negaunee, Lodge 49 in Ludington, Lodge 65 in Greenville, Lodge 100 in Marlette, Lodge 125 in Detroit, and the world's only international chapter, Lodge 184 in Port Huron and Sarnia, Ontario. While times have changed, the essential mission of the Danish Sisterhood in America remains the same: to preserve, share, and promote Danish traditions and culture.[2]

1. Ludvig M. Hoffenblad, *Det Danske Søstersamfund i Amerika in Danske i Amerika*, (Minneapolis: C. Rasmussen Publishing, 1908), 227–32.
2. The Danish Sisterhood in America. President Sindy Poremba. 27 October 2004, http://www.danishsisterhood.org.

Germanization ordered by Otto von Bismarck upon the Danes in Schleswig made a total of sixty thousands ethnic Danes leave the area during the first forty years of German rule.[3]

Early Danish Settlers in Michigan

The first permanent Danish settler in Michigan was a young man named Christian Jensen, in 1853. Previously some Danes had come through Michigan as Great Lakes seamen, but none had settled in the state.[4] Jensen first lived along the Flat River in Montcalm County, eventually reaching Gregory's Mill, now called the Village of Gowen. Jensen quickly Anglicized his name, calling himself Johnson, and he bought a piece of land just north of Gowen. After clearing the land, he sent a positive letter home to Denmark in which he stated, "Here are cheap and plenty of good timber land, good wages, earnest people, good government, nice girls; I am going to marry one of them."[5]

The following year two more Danes arrived, newlyweds August and Ane Rasmussen, on the recommendation of Christian Johnson's letters. In turn, Rasmussen began sending positive letters home to Denmark about the abundant opportunities available in the Gowen area. His very first letter home set the tone for future correspondence:

> My dear brother C. Rasmussen, Relatives and Friends: I will write to you today August 3, 1856, to perform that promise I gave you when I last saw you, namely, write you how we got through our voyage, etc. We are both in life and in good health. We reached C.J. [Christian Johnson] all right. We are living near a river. Here are plenty of sawmills and lots of work. It is now in haying and harvest time here. The wages are about six times as much as in Denmark. As we have not yet received our trunk, we are going to work a little while to earn some money. My wife has a good place with a relative of Mrs. C.J., and C.J. and I go out to work in the harvest field. We can here get a good house to live in, and all the stove wood we need free of charge. Here are thousands of acres of good farming land to be had almost for nothing. Here is more than enough good land for all the people in the country where you live. Here are good and noble people. Think what

The Danish Festival in Greenville

In the mid 1960s, community leaders in Greenville decided to organize an event to promote the city. To help make it a truly community-based project, the public was encouraged to submit ideas, with the winner receiving a cash prize. The winning suggestion came from local resident Mrs. Dorothy Oliver. She believed a festival celebrating Greenville's Danish heritage would be a hit. Mrs. Oliver's guess was correct. The first festival was held on August 18, 1965, and it quickly became a community tradition on the third weekend of August. The very first festival featured a parade to begin the festivities, followed by a soccer game at Black Field, a Danish smorgasbord, fireworks, and two outdoor dances. Included in the activities was a drawing with the grand prize an all-expense-paid Scandinavian tour for two to Denmark, Norway, and Sweden. Since 1965, the Danish Festival has seen explosive growth, but it has avoided becoming a commercial venture. It is a registered nonprofit organization with a governing board consisting of eighteen members and one salaried employee. In 2004, an estimated seventy thousand people passed through Greenville to attend the celebration. The Danish Festival has become one of the largest community-based events in Michigan and one of the largest Danish-themed celebrations in the world.

Visitors to the festival can expect several activities for the entire family. The Grand Dansk parade throughout downtown Greenville highlights the festivities. Other popular activities have included a basketball and softball tournament, a road run, a talent show, an arts and crafts fair, a raffle, the Young Miss Danish pageant, the prince and princess pageant, and various food booths, serving both Danish and American specialties.

a good opportunity you can secure for each of your children, while in Denmark they cannot get a poor shanty. If God is willing, and we live, my plan is to clear a couple acres of land, and seed in with wheat, and build a good log house. I can work at this once in a while, and keep to work for the company most of the time, and thus earn our living and pay some down on the land. Now, it is for you to make up your mind and start out of the old house. I will do my part. Come out, and bring along our brother-in-law, and your wife's folks, and as many as

you can get. We will provide for you all. I hope to see you once more.
Let us soon hear from you and what you will do. According to what
you write, I shall lay my plans. Your brother, A.R.[6]

Rasmussen's bitter feelings toward Danish landowners continued
in future letters, as he wrote that American farmers received better
wages than their Danish counterparts from "those long-fingered, proud
noblemen of Denmark who feed their harvest people on salt herring
and barley pudding seven hundred and twenty times a year."[7] August
Rasmussen's letters had an almost immediate impact, as by the following year, 1857, of the forty Danes who had arrived in Gowen, thirty-six
were his relatives.

The Danes made a living working in the numerous sawmills in and
around Greenville and by farming and dairying.[8] The gently rolling
landscape of southern Michigan is very similar to that of Denmark, so
the Danes immediately felt at home in the state. Furthermore,
Montcalm County's good-quality soil made it easy for the new arrivals
to utilize the agricultural skills they had honed over generations in
Denmark. Corn, wheat, and potatoes grew in abundance, and the positive letters written by the immigrants and read by friends and relatives
in Denmark encouraged even more Danes to pack up and move to
Michigan.

Danish Education in the United States and Michigan

One of the greatest contributions Denmark has made to the world of
education is the folkehøjskole, or the folk school. The movement for
folk high schools grew out of the nineteenth-century nationalist movement in Denmark. The schools were particularly popular in Schleswig,
as the ethnic Danes in the area were under constant pressure from the
Germans to assimilate, even before the area officially fell under German
jurisdiction in 1864. Folk schools catered primarily to students with a
minimal formal education, teaching them the essentials of Danish society, including history, literature, music, and language. Students lived at
the schools for a term, with men commonly attending during the winter so they could tend to their farms during the summer. The purpose

of the schools was not to train the students for any particular job, but rather to make them well-rounded, informed citizens. For that reason, exams were not given and grades were not recorded.[9]

By the time Danes began leaving for the United States in the 1860s, the folk school movement was fully entrenched in Danish society. In the United States, many Danish-Americans sought to duplicate the folk school system they had come to appreciate in Denmark. Two of their strongest supporters were the famous Danish bishop Nikolaj Frederik Severin Grundtvig and his son Frederik Lange Grundtvig. The elder Grundtvig supported the cause and curriculum by writing a songbook especially for the Danish-Americans. One of the songs, *Der er et yndigt land* (*There is a lovely land*), has since become the civil Danish national anthem. The younger Grundtvig traveled to the United States to help start the folk schools. In time, five folk schools in the Grundtvigian tradition opened in the United States in rural areas near established Danish settlements in Elk Horn, Iowa; Nysted, Nebraska; Danebod, Minnesota; Solvang, California; and Ashland, Michigan.

The first Dane to come to Ashland was an eighteen-year-old man named Martin Jensen in 1876. The following year three brothers, Peter, Jess, and Chris Christensen arrived in the tiny south-central Newaygo County community. Within a couple of years, several Danish families made the Ashland area their new home, arriving both directly from Denmark and from other parts of the United States. By 1882, the Danish community in Ashland was large enough to support a folk school. The first director of the Dane College, as it was called, was Hans Jørgen Petersen, who came to Ashland from the folk school in Elk Horn, Iowa.

Petersen stayed in Ashland until 1886, when he moved to Minnesota to open another folk school. Over the next several years, numerous men led the school, including the Reverend Simon N. Kjems. The deed to the folk school property was generally held by the director, so when Kjems unexpectedly died and his widow returned with her children to Denmark, legal ownership of the property was up in the air. Seventeen years later, the situation was resolved and a new director arrived at the school. Keeping a director for any length of time proved difficult, due to a lack of funds and to personality conflicts. Peter Kjolhede served as director on three separate occasions, eventually dying in Ashland in

The folkehøjskole, or the folk school, is a uniquely Danish institution whose influence reached into the Danish immigrant communities in America. The folk schools were a place to study, not toward the goal of achieving a degree, but to become better-informed citizens. Michigan's folk school, located near the Danish community in Ashland, opened in 1882 and existed to teach attendees about music, literature, history, and good citizenry. The school was never a major success, and it changed hands several times before closing for good during the Great Depression. The school's last buildings were torn down in the 1970s. Folk schools remain popular in Denmark. In this picture, several generations of families gathered on the school's front porch for a group photograph. Above them, the Danish word Velkommen *wishes all visitors welcome. (Photograph courtesy of the Clarke Historical Library, Central Michigan University).*

1937. Another man, a bachelor named Reverend N.C. Nielsen, lived at the folk school during one of its closed periods and served the local Danish congregation. He invited himself to dinner at a parishioner's home every evening, much to the chagrin of many of the congregation's women, who suddenly had one more plate to prepare. One evening during dinner, the resentful women secretly descended upon the school and packed up all of his belongings and put them out on the front porch, signaling the end of his time in Ashland.

In 1928, a family of non-Danes from Chicago named Graham bought the school and attempted to re-open and operate it on the folk school model. Almost immediately, it drew attention from urban newspapers touting the folk school experience as a way to "get the most out of your family relations, your job, your community, your leisure hours, and your social contacts."[10] While adults did come to the school in the beginning, it was never financially successful, but its facilities served as an important social gathering point and source of food for the local community during the Great Depression. After ten years, the Graham family moved on and the buildings were again empty. Eventually, the Dane College's buildings were sold and used as a nursing home. In the early 1970s, Grant, Michigan, resident Arthur Nelsen, a son of one of the congregation's founders, acquired the buildings but they were in disrepair. Soon afterward, the buildings were torn down, thus ending the final remaining remnant of the Old Dane College.[11]

Danish Religious Life in the United States and Michigan

Upon their arrival in the United States, contact between the Danish immigrants and their homeland was limited. For many immigrants their only tie to other Danes and Scandinavians came at church. The national church in Denmark was, and still is, Evangelical Lutheran. Most Danes belonged to the national church and sought to maintain this ancestral tie in the United States. Those who belonged to other faiths, especially Mormons, Baptists, and Mission Covenants, were also eager to continue their religious affiliations in the United States.

In Michigan, Danish Lutheran churches soon sprang up all over the state. They were served by a small, yet dedicated, group of pastors. Most of the pastors received their theological training in Denmark, but in time a Danish Lutheran seminary was established at Grand View College in Des Moines, Iowa. Most of the Michigan churches were established in communities with large Danish populations, including Greenville, Muskegon, Ludington, and Manistee. Other churches opened in the small Danish communities of Gowen in Montcalm County, Nunica in Ottawa County, and Brown City and Marlette in Sanilac County.[12]

A particularly colorful pastor, Danish-born Holger Rosenstand, witnessed firsthand the trust Scandinavians placed in their pastors. When Rosenstand arrived in Muskegon, the Norwegian pastor would not allow him to preach in the Lutheran church. The Methodist pastor, however, allowed him to preach, and Rosenstand was pleased to find a "warm enthusiasm for the church" in Muskegon. Later, Rosenstand visited the Danish community in Ludington. When he arrived at the town's Scandinavian Lutheran church, he met a group of Danish men and told them that services would begin as soon as the building was unlocked. This caused quite a stir among the Swedish and Norwegian trustees, who wanted to be sure that Rosenstand indeed was a Lutheran. Upon showing the trustees proof that he was commissioned by the bishop of the Danish diocese of Ribe, he was allowed to enter. However, Rosenstand was not allowed to use any of the church's candles or lights. After the service, Rosenstand asked the congregation if they were in favor of establishing a Danish-only church in Ludington. All of the Danes voted affirmatively; the Swedish and Norwegian trustees voted against it. In time, a Danish church was established in Ludington by Pastor Rosenstand. However, Rosenstand grew tired of the bureaucracy and hard work involved in starting immigrant churches, and he returned to Denmark in 1878.

The greatest pastor to serve the Michigan Danes was not even Danish. Norwegian-born Ole Amble arrived in West Michigan in May 1874 and began one of the longest ministerial careers in the area's history. He worked tirelessly at enrolling new members, planning worship services, planning for the construction of new churches, and even designing his own parsonage.[13] In all, Amble served seven communities: Little Dane Settlement, Big Dane Settlement, Trufant, South Sidney, North Sidney, Kendallville, and the Look schoolhouse. At a banquet recognizing his forty years in Gowen, Amble said, "In my forty years of service, I have had occasion to confirm children, later grant them marriage licenses and marry them, confirm their children, and officiate at their funeral."[14] Amble remained active in the ministry in the area for fifty-three years, finally retiring in 1927 at age eighty with a lifetime lease on his parsonage and an annual pension of $550. He died in 1934 and is buried in Little Denmark Cemetery north of Gowen.[15] The small village of Amble in Montcalm County's Winfield Township is named in his honor.[16]

Danes in the Lumber Industry

Danish immigrants played a major role in the Michigan lumbering industry at the end of the nineteenth century. Three visionary Danes, Rasmus Hanson, Nels Michelson, and Ernest Salling, put Grayling in

Crawford County on the lumbering map with their extensive operations and philanthropy in the northern Lower Peninsula community.

Rasmus Hanson was born on the Danish island of Falster in 1846 and served in the Danish army before immigrating to the United States in 1865. His first stop was in the large Danish community in Racine, Wisconsin. Soon after, he moved to Manistee and began working on the wharf for twenty dollars per month. He soon worked himself up to foreman, and by 1867 he had become involved with Ernest Salling in buying timber, lumbering it, and selling the logs. Within a couple of years, Hanson sold out his interests to Salling. He then went into business with Nels Michelson, forming Michelson, Hanson and Company. In 1873, the name was changed to R. Hanson and Company. Ernest Salling reunited with Rasmus Hanson in 1878 under the name Salling, Hanson, and Company.[17] Hanson was a dedicated Republican, and he attended the 1892 Republican National Convention in Minneapolis. Four years later, he represented Michigan as a member of the Electoral College. Back in Grayling, Hanson sat on the local school board for fifteen years.[18]

Nels Michelson was born in 1840 in Denmark. His path to America mirrored Rasmus Hanson's almost identically, as he, too fought in the Danish war against the Prussians before leaving for America. Like Hanson, his first stop was with family in Racine before arriving in Manistee to work at a lumber camp. It was there that Michelson met Hanson, and the two pooled their $1,500 savings to buy equipment and secure a log-clearing contract. Their operations continued to grow, despite a Manistee bank failure that cost them a significant amount of their savings. They acquired more land and equipment, and enjoyed some success before joining forces with Ernest Salling in 1878.

Ernest Salling was born in 1843 near Viborg on the Danish peninsula of Jutland. Salling did not fight in the Danish-Prussian War, and arrived in the United States in 1862. His first stops were in New York and Chicago before moving to Detroit, eventually moving to Manistee in 1863. He alternated summers and winters by working as a sawmill foreman and working as a superintendent in a lumber camp, respectively. Between 1867 and 1878, he partnered with Rasmus Hanson in a business of buying and selling pinelands. In 1879, Salling sold his business and

The lumber industry drove the economy of central and northern Michigan for decades, until the old-growth trees were depleted and the industry became less profitable. Three Danish men, Rasmus Hanson, Nels Michelson, and Ernest Salling, played significant roles in the development of Michigan lumbering. They were introduced to the business in the sawmills of West Michigan before setting out to the forests of the state's central and northern regions. The Danes chose Grayling as their headquarters, and they imported a significant number of countrymen to work for them. After the lumber industry slowed, Hanson, Michelson, and Salling remained committed to the Grayling community, as evidenced by their numerous philanthropic activities in the area. (Photograph courtesy of the Crawford County Historical Society).

returned to Denmark to visit family and friends and travel throughout Europe. One year later, in 1880, Salling returned to Manistee and re-teamed with Hanson on their largest project to date, Salling, Hanson, and Company.[19]

Salling, Hanson, and Company began its operations in Grayling. At first, they used the Manistee River to transport the logs from their lands to competitors' mills in Manistee. By 1882, the company had acquired its own mill, and a few years later built a better one with a capacity of twenty million logs per year. To feed the new mill, the company acquired over sixty thousand acres of pinelands in Crawford, Kalkaska,

Montmorency, and Presque Isle counties. By 1900, they had opened another facility in Johannesburg in Otsego County, and the company's good fortunes continued.

Thousands of laborers were needed to cut down the trees and work at the lumber mills, and Salling, Hanson, and Company knew just where to get the workers. The company recruited actively in Denmark to attract Danes to Crawford County. Thousands of Danes answered the call. While many left the community when the logging industry ended, Grayling still has one of the largest Danish-American communities found anywhere in the state.

By the 1920s, the logging era of northern Michigan had come to an end. A majority of the virgin pine forests had been cut down, and second-generation pine was not of the same quality as the original. While the timber jobs and profits were no more, the commitment Rasmus Hanson and Nels Michelson made to Michigan and the Grayling community remained. The most significant sign of this commitment was given by Rasmus Hanson in 1913, when he donated nearly fifteen thousand acres of former timber land southwest of Grayling to Governor Woodbridge N. Ferris and the State of Michigan. The land was named Camp Ferris, but was later renamed Camp Grayling, and became a training ground for the Michigan National Guard. In appreciation of the gift, Governor Ferris renamed the large lake on the property Lake Margrethe, in honor of Rasmus Hanson's wife. Michelson's philanthropy was directed toward supporting the spiritual life of the community. Despite his Lutheran faith, Michelson was a major benefactor of the Methodist Episcopal Church in Grayling. He provided support for the Michelson Memorial Methodist Episcopal Church, and after it burned down, for its replacement, the Michelson Memorial United Methodist Church. The latter exists today to serve as a memorial of the generous support Nels and Margrethe Michelson provided to the Grayling community.[20]

Danes in the Automotive Industry

One of the most significant figures in establishing either Detroit's place or Detroit as the world's automotive capital immigrated to Michigan

Danish-born automotive executive William S. Knudsen was undoubtedly the most significant Danish-American in Michigan's history. Knudsen first arrived in the state in 1913 to work at the Ford plant in Detroit. He rose quickly through the ranks at Ford, and after World War I, he built the company's first European plant in his native Copenhagen. In 1922 Knudsen joined General Motors as a consultant, and shortly thereafter he was named vice president of the Chevrolet Division. In 1937 Knudsen was elected president of General Motors. During World War II, Knudsen accepted the commissioned position of lieutenant general with the Department of Defense as director general of the Office of Production Management. Knudsen ended his military service in 1945 and died three years later. (Photograph courtesy of the National Automotive History Collection, Detroit Public Library.)

from Denmark. William S. Knudsen, born Signius Wilhelm Poul Knudsen in 1879 in Copenhagen, completed school in Denmark and trained as a mechanic before emigrating to the United States in 1900. After employment stints in New Jersey and New York, Knudsen arrived in Michigan in 1913 to work at the Ford plant in Detroit. Knudsen rose quickly through Ford's ranks and was soon placed in charge of all Ford assembly plants in the United States. During World War I, Knudsen managed Ford's boat manufacturing activities.[21] After the war, Knudsen was assigned the task of building Ford plants in Europe. Not surprisingly, he located the company's first postwar European plant in his native Copenhagen.[22] Knudsen's record at Ford was remarkable. During his seven years at the company, net sales jumped from 89 million dollars to 687 million dollars.[23]

After a short stint with Detroit's Ireland & Matthews Manufacturing Company, Knudsen joined General Motors as a consultant in 1922, but was soon promoted to executive vice-president of the Chevrolet Motor Division. He held several other high-level positions with GM before being elected president of General Motors in 1937, succeeding the famed Alfred P. Sloan Jr. Knudsen resigned from General Motors in 1940, when he accepted President Franklin Roosevelt's invitation to take a commissioned position of lieutenant general with the Department of Defense as director general of the Office of Production Management. The editors of *Time* recognized Knudsen's work in the war effort by putting his photograph on the cover of the October 7, 1940, edition.

General Knudsen left military service on June 1, 1945, and was awarded the Distinguished Service Medal. He returned to Detroit and sat on the General Motors Board of Directors. Shortly thereafter, he was awarded the Grand Cross of Dannebrog by His Majesty King Christian X of Denmark in Copenhagen. William Knudsen died on April 27, 1948. His life is summarized well on a plaque placed on his birth home in Copenhagen that says, "He was to Denmark a Good Son and to America a Good Citizen."

Sweden

Historical Context for Immigration

Swedish immigrants make up one of the oldest European ethnic groups in the United States. In 1637, Swedish, Dutch, and German merchants created the New Sweden Company to trade American tobacco and furs with Europe. The following year, a hearty group of Swedes and Swedish-Finns reached the Delaware Bay. Over the next seventeen years, several hundred more Swedish speakers arrived in the Delaware River Valley and built numerous productive farms. However, the close proximity of other European powers, most notably the Dutch, made it difficult for Sweden to maintain a sovereign colony in the New World. In 1655, New Sweden was surrendered to the Dutch, but the new Dutch governor permitted a continued Swedish presence in the area. Even a generation later, Swedish culture remained. In 1682, William Penn visited the Swedish community "with churches and schools, law courts and all the other elements of civilization."[24]

Swedes began immigrating again to the United States in the middle of the nineteenth century. Many of these early immigrants were either idealistic, literate men who were irritated about the lack of political reform in Sweden or dissenters from the Swedish state church, seeking their freedom in America. The largest and most visible wave of Swedish immigration consisted primarily of poor farmers who settled in the Great Lakes and prairie states. Later waves of Swedish immigrants chose to live in and help build America's burgeoning cities or to harvest its minerals. In all, one-sixth of the Swedish population, or, approximately one million Swedes, immigrated to the United States between 1850 and 1930.[25]

Many mid-nineteenth-century Swedish immigrants to the United States were pioneers who believed that Swedish society was not progressing fast enough toward a more inclusive democracy, and they admired America's more advanced democracy. The introduction of required military service in their homeland served as another impetus for many idealistic Swedes, especially those who were under twenty years of age, to emigrate.[26] Many early Swedish immigrants chose to live together in communities, primarily in the western Great Lakes and prairie states of Wisconsin, Illinois, and Iowa.

Religious immigrants, on the other hand, opposed the organization of the Swedish Lutheran church and desired a more fundamentalist church. Followers of a Swedish zealot named Eric Jansson built the most famous Swedish religious community at Bishop Hill, Henry County, Illinois. The community was an experiment in theological communism, but was thwarted with the tragic murder of Jansson at the hands of a quarrelsome acquaintance.[27]

The Swedish immigrants who populated the Upper Midwest made up the next wave of Swedish immigration. They left Sweden for several reasons. A growing population and longer life expectancy made obtaining land in Sweden challenging. Additionally, multiple years of crop failures in the late 1860s devastated Sweden and other European countries, making hunger a severe problem. The abundance of arable land and the opportunity to become wealthy on land speculation in the Upper Midwest factored largely in Swedish immigration to that region. The Swedes would often arrive in North America in Montreal and New York and travel by rail to Chicago. From there, they spread out throughout the Upper Midwest, generally by rail and steamboat. Whereas during the 1840s the prairies of western Illinois were a popular destination, an increasing number of these later Swedish immigrants moved north,

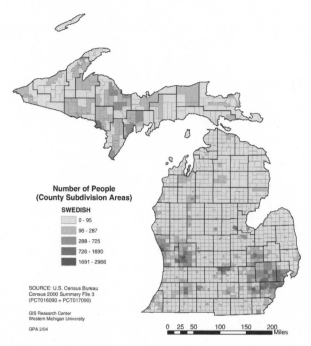

Number of People
(County Subdivision Areas)
SWEDISH

0 - 95
96 - 287
288 - 725
726 - 1690
1691 - 2966

SOURCE: U.S. Census Bureau
Census 2000 Summary File 3
(PCT016090 + PCT017090)

GIS Research Center
Western Michigan University

GPA 2/04

0 25 50   100   150   200 Miles

Distribution of Michigan's Population Claiming Swedish Ancestry, U.S. Census 2000.

to the bountiful, untamed forests, lakes, and river valleys of Minnesota, Wisconsin, and Michigan.[28]

The third wave of Swedish immigrants were attracted to the opportunities available in the growing cities and the bountiful iron mines. The industrial base in Chicago, Detroit, Minneapolis, and Milwaukee provided stable employment for the men in the sawmills, flourmills, textile factories, and later, automobile factories. The women frequently worked as nannies and servants in homes. Others decided to head to the iron ranges of Michigan's Upper Peninsula and Minnesota's Arrowhead. Swedish immigrants were regularly recruited for industrial and mining jobs because employers felt the Swedes were hardworking, strong, healthy, intelligent men.[29]

Swedish immigration to the United States continued through the early years of the twentieth century, but slowed during World War I and did not regain significant momentum during the 1920s. Like other countries, Sweden was severely impacted by the U.S. government's strict immigration regulations, enacted before and during the Great Depression.

The Swedish impact on the Upper Midwest cannot be ignored. Today, Minnesota is the undisputed capital of Swedish America, and the Upper Midwest is recognized in the United States and abroad as the world's most Swedish and Scandinavian region outside of Scandinavia.

Earliest Swedish Immigration to Michigan

Michigan's first Swedish immigrants arrived in the state in late 1853. A small group of Swedes set out from their homeland late that summer, arriving in Massachusetts ten weeks later, in October. The group continued its journey to Michigan, where the members immediately met up with another party of newly arrived Swedes. The two groups joined and spent their first three years in America together in Plymouth, Wayne County. At that time, they continued west and settled near Kent City, formerly Lisbon, in Sparta and Alpine Townships in Kent County, north of Grand Rapids. Many of these Swedes descended from the parishes of Löfby and Svenljunga in southern Sweden near the city of Jönköping. In contrast to most early American Swedish communities, a pastor did not accompany the group to Michigan. The immigrants were deeply religious, however, and left Sweden to avoid the harsh critiques many devout Christians received from the general public and the state church's authorities, who considered them "too religious." [30]

In 1859, six years after the first Swedes arrived in Michigan, a Swedish pastor living in Chicago named Erland Carlsson was asked to pay a visit to the community. Upon arrival, Reverend Carlsson found the community already well established, and he set out to tend to their spiritual needs, including baptizing the children born there. In his notes, Reverend Carlsson estimated that nine or ten Swedish families lived in the community, totaling approximately fifty persons.

The first Swedish immigrants struggled with the same early challenges that faced other newcomers, but by the time of Reverend Carlsson's visit, the Swedes had paid off their lands, built houses, cleared the surrounding forests, and cultivated anywhere between five and twenty acres of land each. The Swedish immigrants had constructed a school and other common buildings, and Reverend Carlsson was confident that the community was in good physical and spiritual health, and was hopeful for its continued success.

Agriculture was the livelihood of the earliest Swedish community at Sparta, and the agricultural skills the Swedes had learned at home in Jönköping paid great dividends upon their arrival in Michigan. Whereas other immigrant communities struggled mightily to adjust to life in the harsh elements, the Swedish colony thrived. For the most part, the community was self-contained, but its close proximity to the village of Berlin, located just eight miles away, meant that the Swedes could shop there and take advantage of Berlin's rail connections to sell their surplus agricultural products in larger communities like Grand Haven and Detroit.

Maintaining a religious life was important to the Swedes. For the first several years, the Swedes worshiped in the home of one of the settlers. This practice continued until 1865, when the community, enlarged by the arrival of new settlers from Sweden and by the births of babies, grew too large to meet in a private home and began meeting at the school. The following year, the colony's church was officially accepted into the Lutheran Synod and named "the Swedish Evangelical Lutheran Mamrelund Union of Lisbon, Kent County, Michigan." Finally, in 1872, the congregation built its own sanctuary.

The earliest Swedish colony in Kent City continued to grow and thrive. In time, the colony would fully integrate into the surrounding non-Swedish communities, and many of its members would leave to pursue interests elsewhere, but its success served as a model for other Swedish communities in Michigan. Two members of this community who went on to make a significant impact elsewhere in the state were Charles Herman Blomstrom and Charles Theodore Grawn. Charles Herman Blomstrom was born into the community in 1867 and went on to operate the C.H. Blomstrom Motor Car Company, one of Detroit's largest automobile manufacturers. The company produced several car models and employed hundreds of workers. Charles Theodore Grawn was born in Plymouth, Michigan, in 1857 and moved to the Kent County colony as a toddler. He went on to attend the

University of Michigan, and became superintendent of schools in Plymouth and Traverse City. Later, he supervised the training department at the State Teachers College in Ypsilanti, now Eastern Michigan University, before being named the president of the State Teachers College in Mount Pleasant, now Central Michigan University, a position he held for eighteen years.

Later Swedish Immigration to Michigan

The greatest wave of Swedish immigration to Michigan occurred during the period of 1870–1900. These immigrants were attracted to the railroads, forests, mines, and arable land of the Upper Midwestern states. Whereas many other immigrant groups were not prepared to deal with the region's harsh weather, Swedish immigrants were well accustomed to the difficulties faced by those living in extreme climates. Swedes were known for their hardiness, so political leaders in Michigan and other states in the Great Lakes region were very interested in recruiting them. Many states, including Michigan, employed people whose sole responsibility was to attract new immigrants. In Michigan, this responsibility was given to the commissioner of immigration.[31] One of the most significant responsibilities of the commissioner was the publication of a book, *Michigan and Its Resources*, which described facts about the state of interest to potential immigrants, including information about agricultural outputs, schools, government, and weather, and a description of each county. Highlights of this book were translated into several languages, including German, Dutch, and French, and distributed to immigrant agents and immigrants already in America, for distribution to friends and relatives abroad. In 1884, the commissioner's office released its first Swedish-language materials promoting Michigan. The response was overwhelmingly positive. Two thousand pamphlets were printed, and almost immediately they were all distributed. In his 1885 report to Governor Josiah Begole, Michigan Commissioner of Immigration Henry Fairbank noted, "several of our northern counties have Swedish settlements, and from every point is heard favorable reports as to the character and citizenship of this people."[32]

The northern counties Fairbank referred to were predominantly located in the Upper Peninsula. Marquette, Menominee, Dickinson, Iron, and Houghton counties were particularly popular with Swedish immigrants. Abundant employment opportunities were the primary draw, followed closely by the opportunity to live near countrymen. Ishpeming, in particular, became recognized for its role as the center of Swedish life in the Upper Peninsula. Work was abundant in the iron mines, and from Ishpeming, Swedes found jobs in many towns on the Marquette Range, including Negaunee, Republic, and Champion. As iron was discovered west and south of Ishpeming, Swedish immigrants followed the jobs to the other ranges, particularly in Iron County.

Other Lower Peninsula villages attracted Swedish immigrants, too. Many found work building railroads. As early as 1870, the Pennsylvania Central; Pittsburgh, Fort Wayne & Chicago; Pittsburgh, Cincinnati & St. Louis; and the Grand Rapids & Indiana Railroads joined a consortium called the Continental Improvement Company to increase their miles of tracks. The GR&I worked at extending its tracks all the way from Fort Wayne, Indiana, to Mackinaw City. As they moved north along Michigan's west coast, the need for quality labor was great, as the working conditions were difficult. The Continental Improvement Company wanted to attract Swedish laborers, so they offered them generous incentives, including deferred charges on transatlantic fares, free transportation from New York to Michigan, guaranteed shelter upon arrival, solid wages of $1.75 to $2.00 per day, and the opportunity to purchase land from the railroad on favorable credit terms at the relatively low price of $5.00 per acre.

To help spread the word of these generous incentives, in 1870 Continental Rail sent a Grand Rapids Episcopalian minister named Dr. Josiah Tustin to Sweden. During his first visit to Sweden, Dr. Tustin convinced several families to relocate to Michigan to help build the GR&I and farm the land. His return visit to Sweden in 1871 was even more successful.[33] One estimate places the number of Swedes emigrating to the United States because of Dr. Tustin at one thousand.[34] A significant number of them settled in Burdell Township in Osceola County, and they named their village New Bleking, after the southern Swedish province. By 1873, New Bleking had been renamed as Tustin, in honor

Dr. Glenn T. Seaborg: From Ishpeming to the World

Michigan's Swedish-American community has produced countless individuals who went on to honorably serve their local and state communities. In contrast, Dr. Glenn T. Seaborg went on to serve the world as a Nobel Prize–winning chemist. Born in Ishpeming of a Swedish-born mother and second-generation Swedish-American father, Seaborg left the Upper Peninsula at age ten with his family to live in California. However, he returned north of the Mackinac Bridge many times later in his life, and he took great pride in his U.P. heritage. When Dr. Seaborg was invited to give scientific lectures around the world, he told attendees that he was from Ishpeming. Not surprisingly, few, if any, people in attendance had heard of Ishpeming. Knowing this, the good-witted Dr. Seaborg would tell them, "I can see by the looks on some of your faces that there are a few people here who don't know where Ishpeming is. Well, let me put your minds at ease: it is right next to Negaunee."

Dr. Seaborg gained scientific acclaim though his work in the laboratories at the University of California, Berkeley. In 1941, Seaborg's team discovered a new element, number 94, which he named plutonium. In 1942, Seaborg was given a leave of absence from Berkeley to move to Chicago and work with other scientists on the famous Manhattan Project. In 1951, at the age of thirty-nine, Seaborg was bestowed with the Nobel Prize. Later, Seaborg served as chancellor of the University of California, Berkeley, and as chairman of the United States Atomic Energy Commission. During his distinguished career, Seaborg went on to discover several more elements, including element 106,

of Dr. Tustin. Tustin's Swedish community continued to grow, and two Swedish churches, one Episcopal and one Evangelical Lutheran, were formed to tend to the residents' spiritual needs.[35] In 2004, the Swedish Evangelical Lutheran Church, built in 1882, joined the Michigan historic registry.[36]

Michigan's foreign-born Swedish population continued to grow throughout the 1880s, before peaking in the final decade of the century. The population had receded slightly by the time of the 1900 federal census, but remained the largest Scandinavian population in the state.

The name of Ishpeming-born chemist Dr. Glenn T. Seaborg has quite literally gone down in the annals of his profession. Element 106 on the periodic table of elements is named Seaborgium, in his honor. Earlier in his career, Dr. Seaborg helped discover a new element, plutonium. Dr. Seaborg later served on the Manhattan Project during World War II, and in 1951 he was awarded the Nobel Prize for chemistry by King Gustav VI Adolf of Sweden. Later, he served as chancellor of the University of California and chairman of the United States Atomic Energy Commission. In 1962 he was named Swedish American of the Year by the Vasa Order of America. Dr. Seaborg died in 1999 at the age eighty-six. He never forgot his Swedish Upper Peninsula roots, and Northern Michigan University's Glenn T. Seaborg Center for Teaching and Learning Science and Mathematics is named in his honor. (Photograph courtesy of Northern Michigan University.)

which was named seaborgium, in his honor, marking the first time an element was named after a living person.

Dr. Seaborg died in 1999 at the age of eighty-six. During his career, he wrote more than twenty-five books, held over forty patents, and was granted more than fifty honorary degrees, from schools such as the University of Michigan, Michigan State University, the University of Detroit, and Northern Michigan University. The latter institution, located near his birthplace, named its new Center for Teaching and Learning Science and Mathematics the Glenn T. Seaborg Center in his honor.[1]

1. http://seaborg.nmu.edu/about/seaborg.html, accessed February 21, 2005.

New Swedish arrivals to Michigan, particularly to its rural areas, slowed significantly after 1900, as work harvesting natural resources diminished. By then, second-generation Swedish-Americans, many of whom still identified themselves with their Swedish heritage, had grown up and sought out their own opportunities. While some stayed near their homes and worked in the forests and mines, many were encouraged to receive an education and enter the professional ranks. Others learned trades and served their home communities. Still others left the rural areas to work in the region's industrial centers.

Swedes in Detroit and the Automotive Industry

Early Swedish immigrants, for the most part, avoided permanent settlement in Detroit, in favor of rural areas in western and northern Michigan. The 1850 United States Census recorded only three Swedes living in Detroit. Forty years later, in 1890, only 196 Swedish-born people lived in Detroit. This figure increased to just 267 people ten years later. Many believe the small numbers of urban Swedes can be attributed to a lack of desire to live in large cities. However, two other Midwestern urban centers, Chicago and Minneapolis, attracted significant numbers of Swedish immigrants. In 1890, Chicago registered over 43,000 Swedish-born residents, and Minneapolis counted over 19,000. Rather than reflecting a distaste among Swedes for urban areas, however, Detroit's failure to attract a significant number of Swedes can be blamed on the immigrants' desire to live near other Swedes in the United States.

The Detroit Swedish population reached 601 in 1910. In the next twenty years, the population exploded. The 1920 United States Census counts over 2,600 Swedes in Detroit; by 1930 this figure was over 4,300. The 1930 tally for Detroit represented almost 20 percent of the entire Michigan Swedish-born population of 23,905. Considering that the U.S. national Swedish-born population had grown by less than 4 percent between 1900 and 1930, Detroit's exponential growth is quite remarkable.

The growth of Detroit's Swedish population corresponds directly with the emergence of the city as the country's automotive capital. A demand for labor and higher wages paid at the factories made settling in Detroit an attractive option. Henry Ford's famous decision to pay his employees five dollars per day sent shock waves through the country, the amount dwarfing the salaries workers earned in other cities. Swedes and Scandinavians were considered intelligent, honest, hard-working men and women and were sought out by employers. Detroit's Swedish population consisted of increased numbers of both persons—often single men—immigrating directly from Sweden, and persons born in the United States of Swedish parentage who moved to the city from other parts of Michigan and the Midwest.[37]

One of the most significant Swedish contributions to the American automobile industry came from engineer Carl Edward Johansson. Born and raised in Sweden, Johansson was a trained cabinetmaker who later went to work in a Swedish gun factory. It was while working in that industry that Johansson came up with a series of standardized metric gauge blocks. He named them "Jo-Blocks," and they quickly became invaluable to engineers in industries that relied upon precision measuring. In 1923, several years after his invention had caught on in Europe and with the United States War Department, Johansson and his gauge blocks grabbed the attention of Henry Ford. Ford met with Johansson in Detroit, and the two became friends. After negotiations, Ford purchased Johansson's gauge blocks and implemented them at Ford Motor Company. Their personal relationship was so strong that Johansson was one of only two people—Ford's son Edsel was the other—who was allowed to enter Ford's office without first knocking on the door. Ford ran into a snag, however, when he tried implementing metric gauges into his imperial machines in the factories. Congress had been discussing for years how to standardize the imperial system against the metric system, but could not come up with an equitable solution. Finally, Ford got so disgusted with the delay that he told Johansson to go ahead without a decision from Congress. Johansson decided on 2.54 centimeters to 1 inch. Johansson's conversion remains the standard today.[38] The Johansson family remained in Michigan after Carl Edward retired, and became respected members of the Scandinavian-American community. His son, the Honorable Edward Johansson, became president of his father's company and later served for many years as the Swedish Consul for the State of Michigan.[39]

Swedish Religious Life in Michigan

Many Swedish immigrants, like their Danish counterparts, found solace and community in fostering a religious affiliation upon arrival in the United States. Most of the Swedes remained active in the traditional Evangelical Lutheran church, but in comparison to Danish and Norwegian immigrants, they were more likely to branch out into other Protestant denominations, usually the Baptist, Methodist, and Evangelical Mission Covenant churches.

Michigan's first Swedish churches appeared in the Swedish communities in Kent County. Most were small, but played a central role in the fledgling communities' daily lives. The churches were a place the immigrants could assemble and practice their shared faith. As the communities grew, so too did the churches. In addition to serving the members' religious needs, the churches became a place to socialize, hear news from Sweden, and teach their children about their homeland. Later Swedish Lutheran congregations formed and flourished in communities such as Ludington, Manistee, Cadillac, Bay City, and Lebanon. As Swedish populations grew in the Upper Peninsula, congregations formed in cities along the Marquette, Menominee, and Gogebic iron ranges.

The Baptist church made inroads in recruiting Swedes in the nineteenth century. Swedish Baptists were dissatisfied with the state-sponsored Evangelical Lutheran church and resented having to pay income taxes to the church. This general dissatisfaction caused many Swedish Baptists to leave their homeland, and the church's followers who emigrated to the United States sought to continue their relationship with it in this country. Swedish Baptists sought the same jobs as Lutheran Swedes, assembling throughout the western half of the Lower Peninsula and along the northern shore of the Upper Peninsula. They opened churches in communities such as Cadillac, Manistee, and Muskegon in the Lower Peninsula, and Marquette and Iron Mountain in the Upper Peninsula. Many Swedish Baptist congregations remain in Michigan, but most have changed their names to reflect their all-inclusive Baptist affiliation.

The Swedish Evangelical Mission Covenant Church has its origins in the religious awakening in Sweden during the second half of the nineteenth century. The church grew out of both Catholic and Protestant ideology and spread quickly throughout the country. Today the Swedish Mission Covenant Church is the second-largest denomination in Sweden, with over 165,000 members. Many of the Mission Covenant followers who emigrated to Michigan came from south-central Sweden and settled near the established Swedish communities in West Michigan and the Upper Peninsula. In recent years, the Swedish Evangelical Mission Covenant Church has had considerable success in diversifying its membership to include non-Scandinavians, and congregations are found in communities throughout the state and nation.

Establishing churches was an important step for many American immigrant groups, including Scandinavians. The churches became a place the immigrants could assemble, practice their shared faiths, and discuss their experiences. Most Scandinavians were members of the state-sponsored Evangelical Lutheran church, and they retained that affiliation in the United States. Some Scandinavians did branch out, however, and became members of other denominations. Those Scandinavians who converted to another church generally chose congregations philosophically similar to the Lutheran church; however a significant number of Danish immigrants converted to Mormonism and moved to Utah. The Methodist, Evangelical Mission Covenant, and Baptist churches attracted many Scandinavian immigrants, and exclusively Scandinavian congregations developed in these denominations. These churches retained their distinctly Scandinavian flavor for many years, but by the mid 1900s most had changed their names and service language to English to accommodate a larger audience. (Photograph courtesy of Temple Hill Baptist Church, Cadillac.)

Swedish-Finns in Michigan

For nearly one thousand years, a vibrant Swedish-speaking population has lived and worked in neighboring Finland. Primarily concentrated along Finland's southern and western coasts, the Swedish-Finns are descendents of mostly fishermen, peasants, and government officials who moved to Finland during the centuries of Swedish colonial rule. While the Swedish-Finns have never represented more than a small minority in Finland, their influence on Finland and Finnish society has been significant. Some of Finland's most recognized politicians and artists were Swedish-Finns, including World War II–era president Carl Gustav Emil Mannerheim, former politician and United Nations representative Elisabeth Rehn, composer Jean Sibelius, and writers Tove Jansson and Johan Runeberg. Today, most Swedish-Finns still live in the same coastal areas they have inhabited for centuries. Nowhere in Finland is the Swedish influence stronger than the Åland Islands, a self-governing monolingual province located in the middle of the Gulf of Bothnia. Finland remains officially a bilingual country, and while the percentage of Swedish-Finns has declined to approximately 6 percent, or 300,000 persons, they continue to hold a disproportionately large amount of political and cultural influence in Finland and represent the country's linguistic and historic connection to its Scandinavian neighbors.

Swedish-Finns began immigrating to the United States during the mid- to late nineteenth century, just like their Finnish countrymen and other Scandinavians. The Swedish-Finns generally followed the same paths as Finnish-speaking Finns to their new homes in America, arriving in North American ports at New York, Boston, and Montreal. Abundant employment opportunities in such familiar occupations as agriculture, forestry, mining, and manufacturing made Michigan an excellent final destination as the Swedish-Finns decided where to build their lives in the United States.

While a majority of the Swedish-Finns in Michigan settled in the Upper Peninsula, many found satisfactory opportunities in the Lower Peninsula. As manufacturing grew in the cities of Detroit, Flint, and Grand Rapids, Swedish-Finns established themselves there. In particular, the automobile factories and suppliers in the cities of Detroit and Flint employed many Swedish-Finns. In Grand Rapids, a few Swedish-Finns found work in the furniture factories. The sawmills of Bay City, Manistee, Oscoda, and East Tawas attracted many Swedish-Finns, but many moved away when the mills shut down. Swedish-Finns also worked at the mills in Ludington and Muskegon. However, when those mills shut down, many Swedish-Finns stayed, as those cities were more successful in developing other industries.

The Upper Peninsula was the destination of choice for a majority of Swedish-Finns who arrived in Michigan. Swedish-Finns inhabited virtually every Upper Peninsula community, but most lived near the coasts and mines of the western U.P. Fishing was a common profession in Ontonagon and Cedarville. As in the Lower Peninsula, many other immigrants found work in forestry and sawmills, especially in Munising, Manistique, Menominee, Thompson, Baraga, and L'Anse. Just like their Finnish-speaking countrymen, many Swedish-Finns labored in the U.P.'s productive mines. The iron mines near Crystal Falls, Amasa, Iron Mountain, Norway, Negaunee, Stambaugh, Ironwood, Bessemer, Ramsay, and Wakefield attracted countless numbers of Swedish-Finns. Further north, on the Keweenaw Peninsula, the copper mines provided work for many Swedish-Finns. They established themselves particularly well in the former copper boomtown of Calumet, with a smaller number living in the twin cities of Houghton and Hancock. Swedish-Finns owned many successful shops in Escanaba and Gladstone, and tiny Metropolitan, in Dickinson County, was regarded as one of the largest Swedish-Finn communities in the entire United States.[40] Logging and extensive commercial fishing opportunities attracted countless Swedish-Finns to St. Ignace, and Brevort, and to Cederburg and Hessel in the Les Cheneaux Islands of Mackinac County. Socially, Swedish-Finns were well represented among the many temperance societies founded in Michigan in the early twentieth century. Religiously, Swedish-Finns were active in both the Finnish Suomi and Swedish Augustana Lutheran synods.[41] Wherever they settled in Michigan, Swedish-Finns distinguished themselves with their excellent skills, strong work ethics, and dedicated civic-mindedness.

Norway

Historical Context for Immigration

A hundred years before large petroleum and natural gas reserves were discovered off the Norwegian coast in the last third of the twentieth century, the geographic remoteness, sparse population, limited natural resources, and unforgiving terrain made Norway little more than a neglected cousin in the Scandinavian mindset. Internationally, Norway had virtually no distinct identity, as the country alternated between Danish and Swedish sovereignty until full independence was granted from Sweden in 1905. The solution for hundreds of thousands of Norwegians was to abandon the land of the fjords for the United States and Canada. The deep impact of emigration was felt in virtually every corner of Norway. In 1860, the Norwegian population numbered just over 1.6 million persons. That figure grew to just over 2.2 million by 1900.[42] In comparison, between the years of 1825 and 1928, over 850,000 men, women, and children left the country. This staggering figure makes Norway the second largest per capita European exporter of humans to North America, behind Ireland.[43]

A study of Norwegian emigration is a study of the country's geography. Norway is a long, narrow country located between the rough North Atlantic Ocean and the rocky mountains of the Scandinavian

Peninsula. Over 75 percent of the Norwegian land area is mountainous. Most of the remaining 25 percent is highly forested. This equation leaves very little arable land, mostly along the country's southeastern coast and on the narrow strips of land between the mountains and the fjords. During the nineteenth century, improved medical technology meant that more babies born in Norway survived to adulthood than ever before, which created great pressures on the scarce land resources. At the time, agriculture was the chosen profession of over 90 percent of Norwegians, but as more people desired their own land, it became increasingly difficult to find property. Between the years 1750 and 1850, the Norwegian population doubled, from 625,000 to 1.3 million. By 1930, this figure had doubled again.[44] Considering that 850,000 persons emigrated from Norway during this same time period, the nation's population growth was truly remarkable.

As in neighboring Sweden, several years of severe crop failures in the 1850s and 1860s contributed significantly to the mass emigration from Norway. The situation was more acute in Norway, as the Norwegian economy was significantly less diverse than that in Sweden. Norway was unable to acquire the necessary foodstuffs, as there was less to trade. Furthermore, it was difficult and expensive to deliver goods to the remote villages along the Norwegian coast and in the central mountains. Fish was readily available to most Norwegians, but it became clear to many of them that their best opportunity for consistent, sustained access to food and economic development lay in North America.

A less-significant, yet real emigration factor was Norway's unique nineteenth-century political situation. For centuries, Norway was in a political union with Denmark, with the seat of government located in Copenhagen. Denmark discouraged the evolution of a distinctly Norwegian identity, and promoted Danish national interests before Norwegian interests. In 1814, Denmark was forced to cede Norway to Sweden as a result of the Treaty of Kiel.[45] While Norway's political situation improved somewhat due to the union with Sweden, the Norwegian people still were not independent of foreign rule and influence. As nationalistic movements spread throughout the European continent, many people in Norway were disappointed that they were

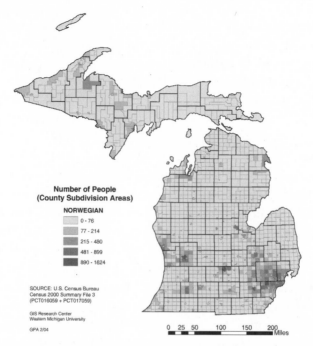

Distribution of Michigan's Population Claiming Norwegian Ancestry, U.S. Census 2000.

unable to gain their independence from foreign rule, and they looked toward the United States as a truly democratic society independent of foreign domination. By the time Norway finally gained its total independence from Sweden in 1905, hundreds of thousands of countrymen had already emigrated.

After 1900, the rate of emigration from Norway to the United States dropped dramatically. Conditions improved in Norway, making the move abroad less necessary. Life improved so much, in fact, that a significant number of emigrants actually returned to Norway. By 1920, fifty thousand Norwegian-Americans had returned to settle permanently in Norway.[46] However, the great majority of Norwegian emigrants remained in the United States. The 2000 United States Federal Census counted 4.5 million people spread across the country claiming partial Norwegian heritage, making it the thirteenth-largest ancestry group in the country, and equaling the entire population of Norway.

The Upper Midwest is the region home to the greatest concentrations of Norwegian-Americans. North Dakota leads the nation with the highest per capita percentage of Norwegian-Americans, at over 30 percent. South Dakota, Minnesota, and Wisconsin also have large Norwegian-American populations.[47]

Norwegian Immigration to Michigan

The first permanent Norwegian settlement in Michigan was founded in Muskegon in 1848. The settlement started out small, but it steadily grew, becoming one of the largest in the state. As early as 1850, the United States census counted eighty-six Norwegians living in Michigan, twenty-seven of whom resided in Muskegon Township. Work in Michigan's logging industry, particularly in Muskegon's numerous bustling sawmills, attracted the Norwegians to the state. Throughout Muskegon County, in White River, Delton, Holton, and Cedar Creek Townships, groups of Norwegians settled and found ample employment opportunities. Michigan's west coast, from northern Allegan County all the way north to the tip of Leelanau County, became the state's most densely populated Norwegian region. The largest Norwegian communities included Ludington, Manistee, and Frankfort. The Norwegian population along the state's west coast continued to grow as lumbering production increased. By 1882, an estimated three thousand Scandinavians resided in Manistee alone, many of whom were Norwegians, working at the city's thirty bustling sawmills and saltworks.[48]

Norwegian farmers also settled near the established Danish communities in Montcalm County. The productive agricultural land was attractive to the farmers who were used to rocky, temperamental Norwegian soil. They were delighted with the high-quality earth in Montcalm County, and they wrote positive letters to friends and relatives in Norway, encouraging them to move to Michigan. Many countrymen eagerly read the "America letters" and set sail for Michigan. As the Norwegians in Montcalm County were in the minority among a significant Danish population, they frequently joined Danish churches and socialized with the Danes, rather than with their countrymen along the state's west.

Alpena, in northeastern Michigan, also attracted a significant number of Norwegians, many of whom worked in the lumber and shipping industries. The Norwegians quickly grew tired of Alpena's rowdiness, however, as there were fifty-three saloons and only three police officers on duty at any one time. Therefore, the community's leaders decided to start a colony of their own. They located a few thousand acres for sale twenty-five miles from Alpena. They purchased the land and named their village Leer, after their southern Norwegian hometown of Lier. Life was difficult in Leer, as the soil and climate in northeastern Michigan was not ideally suited for agriculture. That did not deter their spirits, however, and the settlers formed a local government and opened a school, church, and other community buildings. Over the years, several colonists moved to other Norwegian communities in Michigan, but many stayed in Leer. As late as 1925, over fifty Norwegian families remained in Leer.[49]

Norwegians began settling in the Upper Peninsula during the Civil War after copper was discovered near Portage Lake in Houghton County. Congress passed a law permitting the importation of contract labor, exempt from military service. The Norwegian press was critical of the law and speculated that the Union Army was looking for replacement soldiers. Their suspicions were shown to be justified when, in 1864, a steamer full of 430 Norwegians arrived in Quebec. The Swedish consul learned that about 380 were destined for mining work in Michigan, but the other 50 were headed for Portland, Maine, for service in the Union Army. Therefore, the consul forced the captain to allow the 50 men to come ashore, where he arranged for their safe passage to Chicago. In subsequent years, the Norwegian population in Houghton County continued to grow. By 1880 over 600 Norwegians lived in the county, mainly in Calumet, Quincy, and Hancock Townships.[50]

Later, Norwegian immigrants found employment in the Upper Peninsula's iron mines. Ishpeming was a particularly popular choice. In 1870, only 119 Norwegians lived in Marquette County. By 1876, that number had increased to between 600 and 800. One of the most notable Marquette County Norwegians was a businessman named Frederick Braastad, who went on to serve as Michigan's state treasurer from 1891–92. In 1981, Braastad's descendents donated 238 acres of undeveloped land near Ishpeming to the Michigan Nature Association in his honor.

Other Upper Peninsula Norwegian settlements grew in L'Anse and Skanee in Baraga County. Iron mines near Bessemer and Ironwood attracted Norwegians to Ontonagon and Gogebic Counties, respectively. In the 1880s, numerous Norwegians arrived in Metropolitan, Norway, and Iron Mountain in Dickinson County. Sawmill work brought Norwegian immigrants to Menominee County. Norwegians also found work in Escanaba's sawmills and harbor. Lumbering and fishing brought several hundred Norwegians and other Scandinavians to Manistique in Schoolcraft County and Naubinway in Mackinac County.[51]

Norwegian Religious Life in the United States and Michigan

Most Norwegians belong to the country's state-sponsored Evangelical Lutheran church. Smaller pockets of Roman Catholics, Baptists, Pentecostals, Jehovah's Witnesses, and Muslims are located throughout the country. Non-Lutherans are frequently members of immigrant groups and live in urban areas in southern Norway. As most Norwegians and Scandinavians are only passive Lutherans, immigrants play a significant role in modern Norway's religious life. During the nineteenth century, more Norwegians were active religiously than are today. Most belonged to the state church, but small numbers began converting to other Christian denominations, including the Baptist, Methodist, and Mormon faiths. Norway has a long tradition of religious tolerance, so immigration to North America by non-Lutherans due to religious persecution was rare. One notable exception is a group of 1820s Quakers who were deemed a "menace" and encouraged to leave.[52] A majority of Norwegian immigrants who chose a religious affiliation in the United States remained members of the Evangelical Lutheran church. They believed that a religious affiliation was a key way to remain connected with their ethnic roots and stay in touch with their countrymen.

Wherever large groups of Norwegians settled, Evangelical Lutheran congregations sprang up. Norwegian Lutheran churches appeared in the Lake Michigan coastal towns of Muskegon, Manistee, and

Ludington to serve the area's growing lumber and mill populations. The earliest congregations were primitive, as funds to build churches were in short supply among the newly arrived immigrants. Services were held in private homes and public buildings until congregations could afford to erect their own sanctuaries. Trained pastors were also in short supply, leaving devout laymen to lead the congregations for weekly services and other pastoral duties. Norwegian pastors would travel from Chicago, Milwaukee, and other larger Norwegian settlement areas to Michigan a few times each year to offer spiritual guidance and perform special pastoral services like marriages and baptisms. Over time, the Norwegian churches spread to other communities throughout the state, including Alpena, Marquette-Ishpeming, and Calumet.

The American Norwegian Lutheran church is characterized by a significant number of ideological disagreements, causing numerous splinter synods to form. The three largest Norwegian Lutheran synods were the Hauge Norwegian Evangelical Lutheran Synod, the Norwegian Evangelical Lutheran Synod of America, and the United Norwegian Lutheran Church of America. It was not until 1919 that these three synods agreed to unite to form the Norwegian Lutheran Synod of America.[53] Many Michigan congregations got caught up in the ideological disagreements, and it divided the Norwegian immigrant communities. The union helped alleviate some of the tensions, but Lutheran congregations throughout Michigan and the Upper Midwest continued to struggle with the damage years of doctrinal disagreement had caused. Today, the Norwegian and other Scandinavian Lutheran congregations are members of the Evangelical Lutheran Church of America, the largest Lutheran synod in the country. Many Norwegian Lutheran churches remain in Michigan today, in Muskegon, Ludington, and elsewhere. They have, however, changed their names to reflect their inclusive nature to non-Norwegians.

The Baptist, Methodist, and Mormon churches also attracted Norwegian immigrants, although Norwegian Mormonism was not popular in Michigan. Many of the Baptists converted prior to emigrating, due to dissatisfaction with the Lutheran church. The Methodists' conversion in the United States was based upon an active missionary presence in the Scandinavian communities. Both the Methodist Episcopal

Norwegian Skiing in Michigan

The emergence of skiing as a popular sport in the United States has close ties to the Norwegian immigrants who made Michigan and the Upper Midwest their American home. Archaeological evidence proves that Swedes and Norwegians have used skis for over four thousand years to get around their snowy, mountainous countries. Skiing evolved into a sport in Norway in the 1700s and was firmly established as such when Norwegians began to immigrate to the United States in the nineteenth century, bringing their affinity for cross-country skiing and ski jumping with them. Within a few years, numerous ski clubs were founded in the Upper Midwest, most of them almost entirely made up of Norwegians and Norwegian-Americans. Norwegian dominance of ski club membership lasted well into the twentieth century. Skiing was an opportunity for Norwegian-Americans to identify with their culture, and ski events were often overt expressions of Norwegian nationalism, complete with Norwegian flags, music, and food.

The first ski club in Michigan was started in 1887 in Ishpeming, and was named the Norden Club of Ishpeming. Initially, the club was very popular, but enthusiasm waned in the 1890s. The club was reborn in 1901 with a new, English name, Ishpeming Ski Club, and membership was offered to "men of all nationalities of good character." The decision to appeal to a wider audience was

and Baptist churches were located near the larger Norwegian communities along Lake Michigan and in the Upper Peninsula's iron ranges. They remained distinctly Scandinavian congregations well into the twentieth century, before seeking membership outside the Scandinavian-American communities.

Norwegian Colony in Leelanau County

Michigan's most isolated Norwegian colony was located in Northport and Suttons Bay in Leelanau County. The colony was unique for two reasons. First, Norwegian immigrants generally preferred to live near other large pockets of countrymen, but this was not the case in a wise one, and just four years later Ishpeming was chosen as the home of the new National Ski Association to "regulate club activities and so produce quality in competitions."[1] Norwegian-born Ishpeming resident Carl Tellefsen was named the first president of the National Ski Association. The city, which had excellent ski jumping facilities, was home to numerous successful competitions, including the first official national ski championship in 1905, won by Ishpeming resident Ole Westgaard.

The growth of the National Ski Association has been truly remarkable. Now called the United States Ski and Snowboard Association, the organization has been headquartered in Utah since 1974, and it coordinates the thousands of American skiers vying for spots on the United States Olympic skiing teams. The debt organized skiing owes to Ishpeming has not been forgotten, however. As early as 1938, National Ski Association officials suggested building the United States National Ski Hall of Fame in Ishpeming. The Hall of Fame opened its doors in 1954 and moved to a state-of-the-art facility in 1992. The hall contains exhibits relating the history of skiing, photographs and biographies of accomplished skiers, a gift shop, and the Roland Palmero National Ski Library, the nation's most complete such collection.[2]

1. E. John Allen, *From Skisport to Skiing: One Hundred Years of an American Sport, 1840–1940* (Amherst: University of Massachusetts Press, 1993), 47, 50–51.
2. http://www.skihall.com/history.htm, accessed on December 2, 2004.

Leelanau. Second, whereas most Norwegian immigrants worked in the lumber and mining industries, the Leelanau community consisted predominantly of farmers.

In June 1867, a group of twenty-nine men, women, and children set out for America from the rural western Norwegian county of Møre and Romsdal. Their destination was Chicago, where they had heard of great opportunities. After the long journey across the Atlantic Ocean, the Norwegians continued by ship toward Illinois. Upon reaching the Great Lakes, the immigrants got on the side-wheel steamer "City of Fremont." The ship docked regularly to refuel. One of the stops was at Northport, where the group encountered Gustaf, a friendly Swedish fellow living in the area. Upon hearing that the Norwegians were headed for Chicago, he told them, "This here is the most pleasant place on the earth. There are large forests and many fish. There's good work and fresh air. What in the world are you going to do in that rat hole, Chicago? Stay here, you boys, and chop firewood!" As the Norwegians had already paid the entire fare to Chicago, they continued on to the city. When they arrived there, they discovered that there were few employment opportunities for them, especially since their English-language skills were very poor. Within two weeks, several Norwegians met at their boarding house and discussed their situation. One man, said, "You can do what you like, but I will stay no longer in Chicago. There is no future for us here; besides, I would never be satisfied in this noisy wasp's nest, where every man acts like you have bothered him . . . I'm traveling back to Swedish-Gustaf in Northport on the first boat."

When the Norwegians arrived in Northport, they moved into a cottage near the water. They held a feast—albeit with a meager menu—to celebrate their arrival. Shortly thereafter, they set out to build homes, clear land, and build their lives in Michigan. Within a couple of years, the colony had grown, as relatives arrived directly from Norway, upon receiving favorable letters from the colonists. Most of the Norwegians were farmers, and they raised potatoes as their major cash crop. It was hard work, but there was enough of a market for the colonists to make a living.

Soon thereafter, the Northport colony grew with Norwegians arriving from Alpena. Life in Alpena was challenging, as the soil was poor and the timber profits were diminishing. The Alpena Norwegians sent a man over to Northport to scout out the area, and he returned with glowing reports about Leelanau County's agricultural potential, saying, "this will become Michigan's fruit garden." Several families made the move from Alpena to Leelanau, and played important roles in developing the county's now-famous fruit industry. By 1880, more than 280 Norwegians lived in Leelanau County, contributing extensively to the region's economic development.

Establishing a religious life was important for the Northport Norwegians, and by May 1874, the resident Norwegian pastor in Alpena had visited the community to start a Lutheran congregation. The pastor visited Northport three times per year, and on his second visit, he founded a congregation in neighboring Suttons Bay. There was a bit of tension among the colonists as to the theological direction the churches should take, and eventually they split into multiple congregations in the two villages. Pastor J. Maakestad served the region for an entire generation, performing countless baptisms, confirmations, marriages, and funerals. Today, Bethany Lutheran Church in Northport remains as a descendent of the colonists' Norwegian Evangelical Lutheran congregations.

Access to railroads was vitally important to the Norwegian colonists, as transportation routes to and from the rural Leelanau Peninsula were limited. The colonists used the railroads to travel to Traverse City, and they depended heavily upon rail service to get their potatoes to markets. A series of early twentieth-century disagreements between the rail owners and the government caused the owners to stop service and threaten to dig up the rails and move them to other parts of the state. While the rails were not removed, the government did not operate the railway, leaving the peninsula's residents and products stranded. The Norwegian colonists decided to band together to purchase the railway, and despite the economic pressures of World War I, they were able to sell enough bonds to buy the line. The Traverse City-Northport route became the nation's only Norwegian-owned railway.

The Leelanau County Norwegian colony peaked in the first quarter of the twentieth century with around one thousand inhabitants. Forty residents represented the colony in World War I, with two dying on the battlefields. In time, the colony integrated itself with the local community, and many of its members went on to practice endeavors outside of the colony's agricultural origins.[54]

Norwegians on the Great Lakes

With over 1,600 miles of rugged North Atlantic coastline, Norway and the Norwegian people have always been intimately tied to the sea. For hundreds of years, Norwegian seafarers honed their nautical skills on the unforgiving waters of the North Atlantic as explorers, reaching distant locations in the north and in the New World. By the nineteenth century, Norwegian sailing primarily was limited to a highly successful fishing and merchant marine fleet. Norwegian ships and sailors traversed the entire globe, shipping raw materials and finished products to consumers on every continent. Norwegians were recognized for their sailing skills, and ship owners everywhere actively sought them out to work on their vessels, including on America's Great Lakes.

The first known Norwegian Great Lakes sailors arrived in the United States in the mid-1830s. Most of them settled in Chicago and found employment with local shipping companies. The Norwegians found sailing to be very rewarding financially. Whereas experienced sailors working in the Norwegian merchant marine earned around $19 per month in the mid-1800s, Great Lakes sailors earned from $1.25 to $2.50 per day. During the Civil War, the compensation skyrocketed to $3.50 to $4.50 per day, before settling again to more reasonable wages after the war.

A significant portion of the business involved shipping lumber from ports along Michigan's west coast. Secondarily, the Norwegians manned ships carrying grain across the Lakes. One Norwegian captain from Wisconsin estimated that in the late 1800s the Port of Muskegon handled one hundred million feet of lumber each week, year-round, with forty cargo ships leaving the harbor each day during the sailing season. Most of this lumber was needed to build homes and factories in the bustling cities of Chicago and Milwaukee. Not surprisingly, sailors lived and raised their families in these cities. The sailors took solace in having their neighbor countrymen looking after their wives and children during the extended periods they were sailing on the lakes.

The sheer numbers of Norwegians who worked on the Great Lakes makes their contribution to Great Lakes maritime history significant. In 1870, 516 out of 1,959 sailors, steamboatmen, and watermen living in Chicago were Scandinavians, of which an overwhelming majority was Norwegians. Milwaukee's 400 Lake Michigan workers included 69 Scandinavians. The numbers held steady through the end of the nineteenth century, but there was a significant amount of employee turnover. The expansion of rail services for carrying freight brought shipping prices down, and salaries dropped. Daily wages fell to $1.25 or lower, and many sailors decided that there was no hope for recovery.

They gave up their jobs on the lakes in favor of jobs in the cities or to become farmers in Minnesota, Wisconsin, and elsewhere.

The Great Lakes have long been known for their unpredictable, unforgiving nature, ever since René-Robert Cavalier, Sieur de La Salle's fateful journey in September 1678. On that journey, La Salle's ship, the *Griffon*, sank while on the first recorded Great Lakes cargo voyage. Norwegian Great Lakes sailors experienced the wrath of the lakes on countless occasions, including the infamous November 1913 hurricane.[55] After the four-day storm finished reeking havoc on the Great Lakes, twelve ships were lost, twenty-five others severely damaged, and 250 to 300 men and women had died.[56] Norwegian-American Captain H. C. Hansen of Duluth was sailing in Michigan's waters at the time and recounted the storm:

> I was serving as first mate on the steamer "D.O. Mills," 10,000 tons of capacity, owned by the Interlake Steamship Company, one of the largest steamers on the lakes at that time, commanded by Captain James Jackson. We were on Lake Huron on our way from Buffalo to Duluth when the storm struck us. It began to blow in the evening, and at eleven o'clock at night our steamer was blown upon the rocky shore at Harbor Beach on Lake Huron, so high that there were only twelve feet of water where it was left standing. Huge vessels were whirled around and refused to answer the rudders. Not even the largest steamers could be managed in that storm, as no vessel could stand on the water . . . The only thing that saved us was that we were thrown so high up on the beach. One steamer was found floating bottom up on Lake Huron. It had been loaded with coal, and was found to be the "C.S. Price." The whole crew had perished.[57]

The peak of Norwegian sailing on the Great Lakes occurred in the early twentieth century. At that time, technological advances in the shipping industry required fewer workers, and second- and third-generation Norwegian-Americans followed other employment opportunities. Still, in 1925, 969 out of 22,964 sailors registered with the Lake Carriers' Association were born in Norway.[58] Norwegian labor on the

Icelanders in Michigan

In sheer numbers, emigration from Iceland was just a blip on the radar, with only twenty-five thousand Icelanders living in the United States and Canada at the beginning of the twentieth century, when emigration from Iceland essentially ended. However, considering the small population of Iceland, this figure represents almost one-third of the entire Icelandic population. Proportionately, this makes Iceland one of the world's top immigrant source countries for the United States and Canada.[1] They left Iceland for many of the same reasons as their Nordic brethren, namely famine due to climatic conditions and, amazingly, overpopulation, as there was very little remaining arable land.[2]

Few Icelanders made Michigan their permanent home. However, many groups of Icelanders passed through the state en route to the established Icelander communities in Wisconsin, Minnesota, North Dakota, and especially, Manitoba, Canada. They made temporary homes for themselves in the state, taking jobs and saving up enough money to complete their journeys. In 1872, one such group of seventeen Icelanders entered Michigan from Ontario and crossed the state, eventually taking up temporary residence in Muskegon. In a letter to his parents in Iceland, Arni Gudmundsen described his journey and life working in a lumbering mill in Muskegon, just sixteen days after arrival in North America.

Muskegon, July 31, 1872

My Dear Parents!

We have now been settled for a time in this place in the state of Michigan; we wandered about here and there looking for a place where we could get good jobs, and we think we have now found a suitable one, at least as a beginning. . . .

On the evening of the 18th we went over a river which separates Canada from the United States and runs from one lake into another; we spent the night in the Emigrant House there, together with many Norwegians and Danes. We had now come into our state. . . .

We got work here immediately and the wages are 2 dollars a day or almost 22 marks. We have been here six days. I have worked at night, for these mills run day and night and produce a lot. There are 28 mills in this town, and many shiploads are sent to Chicago every day. . . . The working hours are ten hours

Icelandic emigration to North America never accounted for more than a tiny fraction of the annual arrivals in the United States and Canada. However, considering Iceland's size, the contribution was considerable. Around 25,000 Icelanders lived in North America at the beginning of the twentieth century, a figure equal to one-third of Iceland's entire population. Very few Icelanders relocated permanently to Michigan, but several passed through the state to work at the lumber camps and sawmills to earn enough money to travel to their final destinations in Wisconsin, Minnesota, North Dakota, and Manitoba. A significant Icelandic colony grew in Wisconsin on Washington Island in Lake Michigan. Arni Gudmundsen was one of the Washington Island Icelanders who got his American start in Michigan in 1872. He later became a respected public official on Washington Island. (Photograph courtesy of the Washington Island Historical Society.)

at night and eleven during the day, and it is more pleasant to work at night because it is very hot here—but not so much that we can't stand it. . . .

I do not know how long we will be here, but certainly for the greatest part of the summer. We are all in the same house and we pay 4½ dollars a week for room and board. If we do not miss any days we will thus have 30 dollars at the end of the month, which corresponds to 54 Danish riksdaler, which is quite good. This is an excellent place for good workers, for there are plenty of jobs. . . .

Your loving Son,

A. Gudmundsen

In a later letter, Gudmundsen wrote that he only remained in Muskegon for two more weeks, as he was "somewhat sick from the intolerable heat and the hard work." He eventually joined the Icelander community on Washington Island, Wisconsin, became a U.S. citizen, and worked as a justice of the peace and town treasurer. He died in 1937 at the age of ninety-two, sixty-five years after his short stay in Michigan.[3]

1. Vilhjalmur Stefansson, *Iceland: The First American Republic* (New York: Doubleday, Doran & Company, 1939), 254–55.
2. Jóhannes Nordal, ed., *Iceland 1874–1974: Handbook Published by the Central Bank of Iceland on the Occasion of the Eleventh Centenary of the Settlement of Iceland* (Reykjavík: Central Bank of Iceland, 1975), 31.
3. Conan Bryant Eaton, "From Eyrarbakki to Muskegon: An Icelandic Saga," *Michigan History* 66, no. 3 (May/June, 1982): 13–15.

Great Lakes contributed immensely to the growth and development of industry in and around the entire region.

Norwegians on Isle Royale

Michigan's most remote location was once one of the state's most Norwegian areas. Isle Royale, located over seventy miles away from Houghton in Lake Superior, was home to a thriving commercial fishing operation before residents moved off the island in the years following its authorization as a national park in 1931. The rocky, wooded island with its deep harbor inlets, reminded many Norwegians of their homeland's western fjords. This, combined with the excellent, relatively untapped fishing opportunities Isle Royale afforded, induced a significant number of Norwegians to brave the rough waters of Lake Superior.

Norwegians began arriving on Isle Royale in the 1870s and 1880s. They joined the small numbers of Germans, Irish, English, French Canadians, and Native Americans who fished the island's waters for Lake Superior whitefish, trout, and herring. The maritime and fishing knowledge the Norwegians brought from home served them exceptionally well in Michigan, and by the 1890s, most Isle Royale commercial fishermen were Scandinavians, a majority of whom were Norwegians.

During the first third of the twentieth century, the names of Isle Royale's summer residents read like a Stockholm or Oslo phonebook. Folk named Johnson, Skadberg, Seglem, Hansen, Torgerson, Olsen, Holte, Anderson, Bjorlin, Ekmark, Christianson, Sivertson, Oberg, Lund, Mattson, Knutson, and Edisen lived and worked in all corners of Isle Royale, and contributed greatly to the island's commercial fishing industry. While no exact island fisherman population tally is available, an estimated seventy-five fishing families—totaling about 250 people— lived on the island in the 1920s.[59] At that time, fish were in abundance around the island, and the fishermen were able to provide for their families from Lake Superior's bounty. When the National Park Service took over control of the island in 1931, a great deal of animosity arose between the long-time resident Norwegians and Swedes and the Park

Service employees. Residents were forced to sell their land to the government for next to nothing, and the sturdy buildings used by the fishermen were promptly torn down.

It was difficult to survive life on Isle Royale year-round, so most Norwegian fishermen kept winter residences in villages on the Keweenaw Peninsula and along Minnesota's North Shore and worked on the island during the summer. During the Great Depression, however, the scarcity of off-season work on the mainland forced some families to spend the winter on Isle Royale. Those who remained braved the island's fierce storms, harsh temperatures, and severe isolation. Norwegian-American Holger Johnson was one of the few men to keep his family on the island year-round. Johnson, who had five children, worked as a fisherman and owned a resort for tourists at Chippewa Harbor. To teach the children, the Keweenaw County Commissioner of Schools hired a woman named Dorothy Simonson to come and work on Isle Royale. Simonson kept a diary during her year on the island, and it was published after her death in 1984, giving an excellent account of life on the island, among the Johnson family and the remote island.[60]

By the 1940s, commercial fishing had slowed considerably on the island due to a myriad of reasons, including overfishing and the effects of the dreaded lamprey, and fisherman gave up their jobs for mainland-based employment. While Isle Royale was always one of the least populated areas of Michigan, the Norwegian and Scandinavian influence on the island was great. The specialized fishing knowledge and equipment Scandinavian-Americans brought to the island made commercial fishing a successful endeavor, and helped write an important chapter in the island's storied history.

Norwegian Engineers in Michigan

Rail and automobile transportation between Detroit, Michigan, and Windsor, Ontario, was greatly improved in the twentieth century, in large part because of the ingenuity of two Norwegian immigrant engineers. By the end of the nineteenth century, commercial activities in the Detroit-Windsor area were growing. However, further growth was jeopardized due to the lack of a permanent transportation link between the two cities. Cargo was loaded onto boats and shipped across the Detroit River. Leaders from both sides of the river became interested in digging a tunnel under the river. In 1872, work was begun on a tunnel, but the project was thwarted the following year when the river broke through the tunnel and killed several workers.

A plan to build a fixed link resurfaced in the early twentieth century, and by 1906 construction was underway on a new tunnel for exclusive use by the Michigan Central Railroad. Norwegian-born engineer Olaf Hoff oversaw the project. First, a trench was dug in the river bottom. Next, 260-foot-long sections of twin-tubed steel were assembled on land and towed into the river. The sections were sunk and connected by divers. The work was completed in 1910, and the tunnel was a great success for Michigan Central, and was a vital link in shipping freight between the United States and Canada. Hoff went on to work on other successful projects, including the Harlem Tunnel in New York and the Michigan Central arch bridge over the Niagara River. He died in 1924 and is remembered as a great engineer, with his greatest work being the design of the trenched rail tunnel between Detroit and Windsor.

Less than twenty years later, civic leaders in the Detroit-Windsor area again called upon a Norwegian-born engineer to help solve a different transportation problem, this one involving vehicular traffic. Søren A. Thoresen, a European-trained mechanical and electrical engineer, came to the United States in 1903, eventually becoming interested in tunneling. He arrived in Detroit and set out to design the world's first international vehicular tunnel. The engineering innovation in the Detroit-Windsor tunnel is its lining. Previous tunnels were lined in cast iron, but Thoresen lined his tunnel with structural steel, making it lighter, cheaper, and easier to construct. Fellow Norwegian Ole Singstad, who rose to engineering fame for designing the Holland Tunnel in New York, was brought in to design the Detroit-Windsor Tunnel's complex ventilation system. The tunnel opened on November 1, 1930, and immediately distinguished itself as an invaluable link in the Detroit-Windsor transportation system. The project proved that steel could be used as an effective tube lining, a technique that was applied to other tunnels all over the world.[61]

Conclusions

Very few American immigrant groups assimilated faster and more thoroughly than the Scandinavians. The vast majority of the hundreds of thousands of Scandinavians who made the long journey across the Atlantic Ocean realized that the move was permanent. Thus, they desired to quickly become a part of the diverse American mosaic. Scandinavian immigrants displayed their appreciation for the opportunities the United States provided them by working hard, obeying laws, learning English, and becoming naturalized American citizens. That is not to say that the immigrants forgot their Scandinavian heritage upon disembarkation in the major port cities of the East. Through churches, sports, fraternal and civic organizations, newspapers, and other institutions, Scandinavian immigrants remained in regular contact with each other. What set Scandinavian immigrants apart from many other ethnic groups was the speed with which they became integral parts of the existing majority Anglo-American society. While most were content to work as farmers, loggers, miners, and shopkeepers, many entered various levels of public service, and two ascended to the state's top job. Governor William G. Milliken is a grandson of former Central Michigan University president Charles Grawn, one of the very first children born in Michigan's earliest Swedish community.

Michigan's first female governor, Jennifer Granholm, traces her ancestry to Sweden, and represents a later wave of Scandinavian-American arrivals in the state. Whether working as miners in Houghton, commercial fishermen in Manistique, loggers in Grayling, shopkeepers in Grand Rapids, foremen in Detroit, or governors in Lansing, Michigan's Scandinavian-Americans have distinguished themselves as valuable, important citizens of their adopted state and nation.

Official Scandinavian Representation in Michigan

Denmark

Royal Danish Consulate, David Christiansen Consul, Charfoss & Christensen, 5510 Woodward Avenue, Detroit, MI 48202; (313) 875-9856

Norway

Royal Norwegian Honorary Consulate, Dennis Flessland, Honorary Consul, 26017 Concord, Huntington Woods, MI 48070; (248) 574-6379

Sweden

Royal Swedish Consulate General, Lennart Johannson, Consul General, 7352 Parker Road, Novi, MI 48176; (734) 944-8111

Iceland

Honorary Consulate of the Republic of Iceland, Edward K. Christian, Honorary Consul, 73 Kercheval Avenue, Grosse Pointe Farms, MI 48236; (313) 886-2596

Finland

Honorary Consulate of the Republic of Finland, Gary R. Waissi, Honorary Consul, 1715 Stonebridge Drive South, Ann Arbor, MI 48108; (313) 593-5248

Scandinavian-American Civic and Cultural Organizations in Michigan

Scandinavian immigrants worked diligently to assimilate into American culture. They believed that a key to becoming successful in the United States was to learn the language, customs, and traditions of the majority society. Assimilation did not, however, mean completely turning their backs on their Scandinavian roots. Many immigrants decided to join Scandinavian civic and cultural organizations in the United States to continue to foster a relationship with their ancestral homelands. A majority of the Scandinavian civic and cultural groups in Michigan were branches of similar organizations located throughout the United States. Naturally, most branches were concentrated in communities with significant Scandinavian populations, but some were located in tiny hamlets, far away from larger population centers.

The Vasa Order of America is a Swedish-American fraternal organization. Originally membership was restricted to Swedish-born men, who received help in learning English and the cultural ways of the United States. The organization also provided money during periods of illness, and a death benefit to cover final expenses. Today, the Vasa Order of America has nearly three hundred lodges and is open to Nordic men and women and their spouses who want to rediscover the tradi-

December 13, the feast day of Santa Lucia, is celebrated throughout Sweden and Scandinavia. Santa Lucia Day has its historical roots in Italy, but it has become especially popular in the North, where Lucia, in her crown of candles, brings light to the dark Nordic winters and represents the beginning of the Christmas season. Today, one of the greatest honors a Swedish girl can receive is to lead a Lucia pageant. Santa Lucia pageants are a traditional part of most Scandinavian-American Christmas celebrations. This pageant, sponsored by the Swedish American Heritage Society of West Michigan in Grand Rapids, is one of the nation's largest. Society members Kerstin Trowbridge and Doris Anderson don traditional Swedish costumes, while 2004's Santa Lucia, Swede Kristina Stenström wears the traditional crown of candles, white robe, and red belt. (Courtesy of the Swedish American Heritage Society of West Michigan.)

tions of their forefathers. In Michigan, five lodges operate today. The FRAM lodge in Farmington is Michigan's oldest continuously operating chapter. Other lodges are located in St. Joseph, Muskegon, Portage, and Waterford.[1]

Many Scandinavian-Americans in West Michigan foster a link with Scandinavia through membership in the Swedish American Heritage Society of West Michigan. A small group of Grand Rapids–area residents, led by Doris and Clarence Anderson, decided to pursue organizing a Scandinavian society. The first informational meeting was such a success that the society was immediately formed. Today, it's one of the nation's largest Swedish societies, with nearly four hundred active members. The society meets several times each year to celebrate Scandinavian heritage with traditional Valborg, Midsummer, and Santa Lucia observations. Norwegian-Americans look to the Sons of Norway for a cultural link to the land of their forefathers. The Sons of Norway was founded in 1895 in Minneapolis as an organization to celebrate Norwegian literature, music, and art, and provide financial security to its members. Originally, members needed to be male and Norwegian either by birth or by ancestry, be morally upright and in good health, and be between twenty and fifty years old. The Sons of Norway quickly spread throughout Minnesota, Wisconsin, Iowa, Illinois, and the Dakotas. Today, Sons of Norway lodges are found throughout the world, with membership topping 66,000.[2] Michigan is home to six Sons of Norway lodges, spread throughout the Lower Peninsula in Farmington Hills, Portage, Lansing, Muskegon, Auburn Hills, and Suttons Bay. Michigan's lodges have names commemorating locations in Norway such as Sognefjord and Nordkap, the Norwegian ship *Christian Radich*, and Norwegian gold medal Olympian and Hollywood actress Sonja Henie. Michigan's Sons of Norway lodges celebrate Norway through a variety of activities, including traditional codfish suppers, *Syttende Mai* Norwegian Constitution Day festivals, and Christmas bazaars and parties.

In addition to local Vasa, Danish Sisterhood, and Sons of Norway lodges, Scandinavian-Americans in the Detroit area have an abundance of organizations through which to connect with Scandinavia. The Swedish Club of Metropolitan Detroit in Farmington Hills is an umbrella organization sponsoring a variety of important activities. Some of the most significant activities include the Arpi Swedish Male Chorus, the Scandia Women's Chorus of Michigan, the Senior Danes, and Swedish-language classes.

1. http://www.vasaorder.com/aboutorg.htm, accessed January 31, 2005.
2. http://www.sofn.com/aboutus/History.html, accessed February 18, 2005.

Scandinavian Place Names in Michigan

n the late nineteenth century, countless brand-new villages were carved from the forests of the vast American northern tier. One of the major steps to being granted a post office—and thereby a link to the outside world—was to officially name the settlements. Regularly, village founders decided to immortalize themselves by lending their own names to the communities. Another popular choice was to memorialize locations in Europe by naming villages in the United States in their honor. Scandinavian-Americans were especially adept at following these two models. Throughout the Upper Midwest, dozens of rural communities borrowed names from local Scandinavian immigrants and from cities and hamlets in Scandinavia.

In Michigan, the majority of Scandinavian place names are found in the Upper Peninsula, as prime communities in the Lower Peninsula were already plotted and named by the time Scandinavian immigration reached its peak. The following is a list of Michigan communities, past and present, with Scandinavian names. Most of the information comes from Walter Romig's book, *Michigan Place Names: The History of the Founding and the Naming of More than Five Thousand Past and Present Michigan Communities* (Grosse Point, Mich.: Walter Romig Publishing, 1973).

Amble, Montcalm County. Named in honor of the long-time Norwegian-born pastor of the Danish Lutheran churches in the county.

Bergland, Ontonagon County. Named after Gunlak A. Bergland, a Milwaukee man who built a sawmill in the community in 1900.

Brevort, Mackinac County. Named after a surveyor named Henry Brevort. The name was also given to a local lake, township, and river. Brevort became one of the purest Swedish communities in Michigan.

Carlshend, Marquette County. Named after the village's first postmaster, Charles Peter Johnson, around 1893. Johnson, who was born under the name Karl Petros Janssen, submitted the name Carlslund (Carl's Grove), but the application was returned as Carlshend.

Carlson, Baraga County. Named after the area's first European settler, Swede Nicholas Alfred Carlson, in 1875. Soon thereafter, many more Swedish farmers arrived in the community.

Denmark, Montcalm County. Located along the Detroit, Lansing & Northern Railroad, the station was a popular stop for Danish immigrants.

Dukes, Marquette County. Alternatively called Dukes, Lawson, and Lehtola by the Finns, Dukes was a stop on the Lake Superior & Ishpeming Railroad.

Eklund, Schoolcraft County. Alternatively called Walsh, Eklund was a station on the Detroit, Mackinaw & Marquette Railroad and was named after the village's first postmaster, Nels A. Eklund.

Grawn, Grand Traverse County. Originally laid out by James R. Blackwood and named in his honor, the village was renamed Grawn, which means "pine tree" in Swedish.

Hessel, Mackinac County. Founded by Swedish immigrant John Hessel and Norwegian immigrant John A. Johnson. Hessel worked as a storekeeper and became the village's first postmaster.

Hogstrom, Marquette County. Named after local residents Louis and Lydia Hogstrom, who were the community's general store owner and first postmaster, respectively.

Leer, Alpena County. Norwegian settlement named after the hometown of many of the settlers, Lier, in southeastern Norway.

Norway, Dickinson County. Orginally called Ingolsdorf, the village was founded by Norwegian Anton Odell when his mine's test pit sank. A year later, a sawmill was built there. Norway was originally located in Menominee County, but became a part of Dickinson County upon its creation in 1891.

Juhl, Sanilac County. Named after Danish immigrant Jens C. Juhl, who arrived in town directly from Denmark with his wife and six children. Juhl became a large Danish community with around one hundred Danish families.

Michelson, Roscommon County. Named after lumber baron Nels Michelson. The settlement was located around Michelson's mills and was a stop on the Grand Rapids & Indiana Railroad.

New Bleking, Osceola County. Named after the southeastern Swedish region of Blekinge, the village was settled by Swedish immigrants. It was later renamed Tustin, after Josiah P. Tustin, a pastor in the community.

Olson, Midland County. A rural post office that existed from 1899 to 1913. The second postmaster was a local Scandinavian-American shopkeeper, L. P. Larsen.

Oskar, Houghton County. Named in honor of Oskar Eliasson, a Swedish-Finn. Eliasson came to Houghton County around 1870 and became involved in the charcoal business. He was also the village's first postmaster.

Otto, Oceana County. Named after Norwegian-born settler Otto Brady. Otto was renamed Reed after its first postmaster, Elnathan Reed. It was later renamed again Ferry. Otto Township remains in Oceana County.

Poulson, Mason County. Once a village in Victory Township. Its first postmaster was a Scandinavian immigrant named Rasmus Lykkeby.

Rasmus, Crawford County. Named in honor of Danish lumber baron Rasmus Hanson, who donated the land on which Camp Grayling was built, Rasmus was located on the Michigan Central Railroad between Grayling and Camp Hanson. The nearby Lake Margrethe is named after Hanson's wife.

Skandia, Marquette County. Founded by Swedish and Norwegian immigrants, Skandia was once one of Michigan's purest Scandinavian communities. Its name means "little Scandinavia."

Skanee, Baraga County. Founded in 1870 by Captain Walfred Been, who arrived in the area to escape a storm on Huron Bay and stayed because he liked the land. He named the village after Skåne, his home province in far southern Sweden.

Swedetown, Houghton County. Located three miles north of Hancock, Swedetown was built by the Quincy Mine company to house the large number of Swedish immigrants the company had recruited to work in its mines. However, most of the Swedes either were drafted into the Civil War or were paid replacement soldiers for those looking to escape the draft.

Walhalla, Mason County. Originally named Manistee Junction, a local admirer of Wagner's opera *Die Valkyrie* renamed the village Walhalla, which is the name of the god Odin's hall in Norse mythology.

Yalmar, Marquette County. Named for Swedish immigrant Hjalmar Bahrman, Yalmar was settled shortly after the Civil War. In Swedish, the letters 'Hj' are pronounced like the English 'Y.'

Scandinavian Newspapers in Michigan

Beginning in the late nineteenth century and continuing through the first third of the twentieth century, one of the primary ways American immigrant groups communicated with each other was through newspapers. Most often these newspapers were published locally and had a circulation of a few thousand. The newspapers contained both information of specific interest to the immigrant groups and news from the majority American society. In their earliest years, immigrant newspapers were written almost exclusively in the native language. As the years progressed and the immigrants' familiarity with English improved, and as their children predominantly spoke and read English, the newspapers began publishing in that language. In the later years of the immigrant newspaper heyday, English was the dominant language of print, with only select stories written in the immigrant languages. Not surprisingly, immigrant newspapers frequently went out of business or were sold, as it was very difficult for publishers and investors to make a profit in the industry.

Scandinavian-language immigrant newspapers followed the national trends very closely. The earliest newspapers began publication in the last thirty years of the nineteenth century and were targeted at the larger Scandinavian communities in urban areas and in the Upper Midwest. Early Scandinavians in Michigan relied upon these newspapers, often originating in Chicago or Minneapolis, for news relating to their homelands. As the Michigan communities grew, the demand for locally published newspapers increased, particularly in the Swedish communities. At one time, out of 650,000 Swedish-born people in the United States, 250,000 subscribed to a Swedish-language newspaper. At least sixteen Swedish-language newspapers were published in Michigan, evenly distributed between the upper and lower peninsulas. In the Upper Peninsula, two newspapers were published in Iron Mountain, the *Michigan Veckoblad* and *Monitor*; in Ironwood, *Frihet* and *Ledstjärnen*; in Ishpeming, *Superior Posten*; in Marquette, *Svenska Posten*; in Manistique, the *Härold*; in Munising, the *Munising Tribun*; and in Calumet, *Calumet Posten*. In the Lower Peninsula, there were three newspapers each in Grand Rapids and Muskegon. In Grand Rapids, there was *Michigan Posten, Svenska Michigan-Journalen,* and *Svenska Veckoblad*; in Muskegon, *Fäderneslandet, Frihetsbaneret,* and *Michigan Posten.* Other newspapers included Manistee's *Nordens Medborgare* and Cadillac's *Arbetaren.* By 1938, only one Swedish-language newspaper remained in Michigan, Ironwood's *Ledstjärnen.*

Danish and Norwegian immigrants were less successful at developing their own press. Greenville was home to Michigan's only Danish-language newspaper, *Dansk Folkeblad,* which began in 1895. Many Norwegians relied upon either the local Swedish newspapers or the many Norwegian newspapers published in Wisconsin and Minnesota, reducing the market for purely Norwegian-language newspapers. One Michigan-based Norwegian newspaper, a religious weekly named *Evangeliets Sendebud,* was published in Battle Creek for a few years before moving to Nebraska.

In the late 1930s, two Detroit-based publishers released English-language periodicals, intent upon reviving the Scandinavian press to serve the state's pan-Scandinavian communities. Named the *Norse News* and the *Scandinavian Record,* neither publication was successful, and they both ceased publication within several years' time. Today, just a handful of Scandinavian-American newspapers remain. For bilingual news from Sweden and Swedish America, see *Nordstjernan* or *Svenska Amerikanaren Tribunen*. For Danish and Danish-American news, see *Den Danske Pioneer* or *Bien*. News from Norway and Norwegian America appears in the *Norway Times* and the *Western Viking*.

Scandinavian-American Cooking

To most outsiders, Scandinavian cuisine is seen as bland and without great international appeal. Traditional Scandinavian cuisine is made from simple, hearty ingredients that can survive in the region's rough landscapes and short growing seasons. It was these simple foods, including fish, mutton, pork, potatoes, cabbage, dairy products, and eggs that Scandinavian immigrants continued to make use of upon their arrival in North America. While some of the foods have become a part of American cuisine, most famously the Swedish smorgasbord and meatballs, few Scandinavian foods have made a tangible impact in the United States. Today, traditional Scandinavian dishes are generally reserved for Scandinavian-Americans, who prepare them for family gatherings and holidays as a way to reconnect with their heritage.

Producing a cookbook has long been a popular fund-raiser for churches and civic organizations. Drawing upon the best recipes of the members, the cookbooks are cheap to produce and easy to sell. In 1929, the Ladies' Aid Society of the Scandinavian Methodist Episcopal Church in Ludington released the second edition of its cookbook, *New and Old Tested Recipes*, as a way to generate revenue for a new church planned for the corner of Washington Avenue and Danaher Street in

Ludington. The following are a few of the many recipes for Scandinavian fare found in the book's pages.

Norwegian Lutefisk (Cod Fish in Lye)

Fill a 25 lb. flour sack with hard wood ashes, immerse in cold water (3 or 4 pails) in boiler and let boil 2 hours. Remove sack of ashes and let water stand till clear then pour into basin and put in lute fish. Let fish soak til swelled to natural size, or until it is firm like fresh fish. Remove to jar of fresh water. It is now ready for use. Change fresh water every day until fish has been used up. *(Submitted by Mrs. Soren Ericksen.)*

Rullepølse (Rolled Meat)

Lay two pounds of veal flank flat on a table. Chop or slice one onion finely, spread over veal. Add one teaspoon black pepper and one teaspoon salt. Roll and sew tightly like sausages. Boil about two hours or till done, in water with a little salt. *(Submitted by Mrs. J. Lageson.)*

Medisterpølse (Danish Sausage)

Ingredients: Twelve pounds pork from shoulder, six good-sized onions, two teaspoons pepper, three teaspoons allspice, one teaspoon cloves, three pints stock. Mix all well, keep stirring for about ½ an hour. Then it is ready for sausage cases. Make lengths about fifteen inches long. Tie ends. These sausages can be kept in a weak solution of brine for weeks. *(Submitted by Mrs. Niels Larson.)*

Sylta (Swedish Head Cheese)

Cook five pounds veal shanks and two pounds pork shank with salt and whole allspice until done; strain juice. Take meat and grind it, removing all bone. Add onion and pepper and a teaspoon sugar, add to strained juice. Cook slightly and put in open dishes to jelly. *(Submitted by Mrs. A. Boline.)*

Grønkål (Kale Soup)

Boil, then chop or put through food grinder enough green kale leaves to make about two or three cupfuls. Add one cup diced carrots, one onion, one tablespoon finely cut parsley, two pounds of lean fresh pork, and one pound of salt pork. Let all ingredients boil for 2½ hours. Then add two-thirds cup rice and a little pepper to taste. Let all boil till rice is done and serve.

Julekage (Norwegian Christmas Bread)

Take one quart milk, scald it and let cool. Add yeast and enough flour to make a sponge. Let it rise. Take two cups of sugar, ½ teaspoon powdered cardamom seed, two cups of butter, one cup of raisins, ½ cup ground or finely cut citrus peel, one tablespoon salt, and two or three eggs. Mix all well. Add enough flour and mix like bread. Let rise and put in loaves. Brush tops with one beaten egg. *(Submitted by Mrs. Steffen Nerheim.)*

Brune Kager (Brown Cookies)

Mix one cup of lard, two eggs, one-half cup molasses, one teaspoon ginger, one teaspoon cinammon, a pinch of salt, one teaspoon soda, and three tablespoons of hot water. Roll ingredients in flour and bake. *(Submitted by Mrs. Harry E. Johnson.)*

Fattig Mands Kager (Poor Man's Cookies)

Take twelve eggs (remove five egg whites), twelve tablespoons sweet cream, twelve tablespoons sugar, ½ cup melted butter, and flour. Roll very thin; cut into any desired shape, and fry in hot grease. When cold, sprinkle with powdered sugar. *(Submitted by Mrs. J. Lunde.)*

Flødegrød (Cream Porridge)

Boil one quart of cream and two quarts of milk. Sift flour into the liquid, stirring all the time until it thickens. Add butter about the size of an egg and salt to taste. Serve with sugar and cinnamon. *(Submitted by Mrs. Carl Ericksen.)*

For more traditional Scandinavian recipes—in more manageable portions—see *Scandinavian Cooking* by Beatrice A. Ojakangas.[1] For many traditional Scandinavian recipes with a modern twist and some entirely new ones, see *Kitchen of Light* by Norwegian chef Andreas Viestad.[2]

1. Beatrice A. Ojakangas, *Scandinavian Cooking,* (Minneapolis: University of Minnesota Press, 2003).

2. Andreas Viestad, *Kitchen of Light: New Scandinavian Cooking with Andreas Viestad* (New York: Artisan Press, 2003).

Scandinavian-American Folk Humor

Both native Scandinavians and Scandinavian-Americans have a long, storied tradition of making jokes about each other. Frequently, the tales contain the fictional characters Ole and Lena, and they play upon common stereotypes about stubborn Norwegians and idiot Swedes. The jokes are almost always in good fun, and the characters are interchangeably Norwegian or Swedish, depending upon who tells them. Their legacy is enduring. Over one hundred years after the end of the Scandinavian immigration period, the jokes are still told throughout Michigan's Upper Peninsula, Wisconsin, and Minnesota, and constitute the largest body of folk humor in the Upper Midwest.* The following is one of many Scandinavian-American jokes told in Michigan:

> It is customary in the Northern Peninsula of Michigan when they have a successful season and all the lumberjacks are paid off to request a certain number of the logging camp to stay in camp and take care of the horses and to get the camp ready for the next season.

On one occasion, the boss recognized that the boys had to have some time off on the Fourth of July. A day or so before the Fourth, he talked to Ollie, one of the Swedish boys. He told them that he was planning a "call off" for the Fourth and that he had brought the liquid for the celebration. Celebrations in such a camp are often rather violent. There is a constant controversy between the Swedes and Norwegians as to which nationality is superior.

As the celebration proceeded, the argument waxed hot. Ollie became very angry. He pulled a neck yoke from the wall and threw it around the room. The next morning when the boys recovered, there were two dead Norwegians on the floor. So Ollie took them, dragged them down to the creek and threw them in, and watched them float down with the logs.

About two years later, his conscience began to bother him. They had just elected a Swede as sheriff of the county. Ollie decided to go in and talk to the sheriff about it. He went to the office and said, "Har, Swanson, you ban sheriff har now. Har about two yars ago on da Fort of Yuly vay ban havink an argument on da camp as vich is da best—da Norvaagians or da Svedes—an' I vent an gat me kind 'o mad and I proke a nack yoke, an' da nax' mornink day foun' tvo of dem Norvaagians dead on da floor, an' ay ban takink dem down to de crick and ban trowink dem in, an' vat vay ban going to do about dat?"

The sheriff said, "Ollie, ay only ban sheriff har 'bout sax month. Ay don' know all 'bout das har laws, vay better go see Carlson. Carlson is County Clark. He ban County Clark for five, sax years—he knows all das har laws."

So they went to see Carlson. Carlson said, "Val, yentlemen, vay never had no monkey bassness in das har county like dis. Ay tank ve better take a few days an' look op das har laws. You come back in a few days. Ay'll put dat down on paper an' vay vill fix it op."

When they returned some days later, the sheriff asked. "Val, Carlson, vat did yu find about das har bassness?"

Carlson became serious. "Yentlemen, ay vant to tal yu something. Vay got fafty law books har, an' ay ban readink all das har laws. Vay don't pay no bounty on Norvaagians!"[2]

1. James P. Leary, *So Ole Says to Lena: Folk Humor of the Upper Midwest* (Madison: University of Wisconsin Press, 2001), 62.

2. Donald D. Kinsey, *Drill Cores: Folklore of Michigan's Upper Peninsula*, unpublished manuscript from the collection of Walter F. Gries, Clarke Historical Library, Central Michigan University, 1959.

Notes

1. George R. Nielsen, *The Danish Americans* (Boston: Twayne Publishers, 1981), 32–33.
2. Ibid., 59–69.
3. Frederick Hale, *Danes in North America* (Seattle: University of Washington Press, 1984), xiv.
4. Nielsen, *Danish Americans*, 108.
5. Augustine M. Robertson, *Indians Sawmills and Danes: The Early History of the Flat River Area of Michigan* (Greenville, Mich.: Flat River Historical Society, 1971), 58.
6. August Rasmussen, *Pioneer Life in the Big Dane Settlement* (Blair, Nebr.: Danish Lutheran Publishing House, 1904), 8–9.
7. Nielsen, *Danish Americans*, 108.
8. Alice Stengren, "A Danish Settlement in Grant, Michigan," Unpublished ms., Clarke Historical Library, Central Michigan University, 1970.
9. Nielsen, *Danish Americans*, 176–77.
10. "Learn the Art of Living at Folk Schools: How Vacationists Have Mixed Knowledge With Sunshine at Meetings in Michigan," *Detroit News*, Metropolitan Section, 2 September 1928.
11. Arthur Nelsen, Unpublished memoirs of the Dane College, March 2004.
12. Enok Mortensen, *The Danish Lutheran Church in America: The History and*

Heritage of the American Evangelical Lutheran Church (Philadelphia: Board of Publication of the Lutheran Church in America, 1967), 58, 303.

13. Settlement Lutheran Church, Gowen, Michigan, *Centennial Anniversary 1873–1973* (Gowen, Mich.: Settlement Lutheran Church, 1973).

14. John Dasef, *History of Montcalm County, Michigan, Its People, Industries and Institutions: With Biographical Sketches of Representative Citizens and Genealogical Records of Many of the Old Families* (Indianapolis: B. F. Bowen and Co., 1919), 354–55.

15. Settlement Lutheran Church, Gowen, Michigan, *Centennial Anniversary*.

16. Walter Romig, *Michigan Place Names: The History of the Founding and the Naming of More Than Five Thousand Past and Present Michigan Communities* (Grosse Point, Mich.: Walter Romig Publishing, 1973), 23.

17. *Men of Progress of Michigan: Embracing Biographical Sketches of Representative Michigan Men with an Outline History of the State* (Detroit: Evening New Association, 1900), 409, 412, 438.

18. Bruce W. Carlson, *History Along the Highways of America: Grayling* (Midland, Mich.: Pendell Publishing Company, 1973), 27.

19. *Men of Progress of Michigan*, 409, 412, 438.

20. *The First Hundred Years: An Introduction to the History of the Grayling Area* (Grayling, Mich.: Grayling Area Centennial Committee, 1972), 27–39.

21. Christian T. Feddersen, *Scandinavians in Michigan: With Special Reference to Detroit and Environs* (Romeo, Mich.: self-published, 1968), 123.

22. Norman Beasley, *Knudsen: A Biography* (New York: Whittlesey House, 1947), 96.

23. Ibid., 117.

24. Amandus Johnson, "Colonists," in. *Swedes in America 1638–1938*, ed. Adolph B. Benson and Naboth Hedin, 5–34 (New Haven, Conn.: Yale University Press, 1938).

25. Eric Englund, "Farmers," in *Swedes in America 1638–1938*, ed. Adolph B. Benson and Naboth Hedin, 80 (New Haven, Conn.: Yale University Press, 1938).

26. Ibid., 82.

27. Kendric Charles Babcock, *The Scandinavian Element in the United States* (New York: Arno Press, 1969), 54–59.

28. John G Rice, "The Swedes," in *They Chose Minnesota: A Survey of the State's Ethnic Groups*, ed. June Drenning Holmquist, 248–54 (St. Paul: Minnesota

Historical Society Press, 1981).

29. Ibid., 258–60.

30. C. E. Hoffsten, *The Swedish Element in America: A History of Swedish-American Achievements from 1638 to the Present Day,* 2nd ed., vol. 4, *Swedish American History in Lower Michigan* (Chicago: Swedish-American Biographical Society, 1934), 27.

31. Florence F. Janson, *The Background of Swedish Immigration 1840–1930* (Chicago: University of Chicago Press, 1931), 257.

32. Henry W. Fairbank, *Report of the Commissioner of Immigration for the State of Michigan for the Years 1883 and 1884* (Lansing: W.S. George and Co., State Printers and Binders, 1885), 9.

33. Nils William Olsson, "The Swedish Settlement of Tustin, Michigan," *Swedish Pioneer Historical Quarterly* 12, no. 3 (July 1962): 109–13.

34. Franklin Campbell Smith, *The Diocese of Western Michigan* (Grand Rapids: Diocesan Historical Commission, 1948), 273.

35. Olsson, "The Swedish Settlement of Tustin, Michigan," 113.

36. "History Fans Push for More Markers for Western Sites," *Capital News Service, Michigan State University School of Journalism,* 2 April 2004.

37. Clarence H. Johnson, Origins, "Population, Locations, Occupations and Activities of the Swedes in Detroit" (master's thesis, Wayne State University, 1940), 24–32.

38. Göran Ahlström, "The Edison of Sweden: c.e. Johansson and the 'Standards of Standard, '" *Lund Papers in Economic History* 71(2001): 1–14.

39. Feddersen, *Scandinavians in Michigan,* 51–52.

40. Carl J Silfversten, *Finlandsvenskarna i Amerika: Deres Materiella och Andliga Strävanden* (Duluth: Self-published, 1931), 97–107.

41. Armas K. E. Holmio, *History of the Finns in Michigan* (Detroit: Wayne State University Press, 2001), 407–10.

42. Theodore C. Blegen, *Norwegian Migration to America, 1825–1860* (Northfield, Minn.: Norwegian-American Historical Association, 1931), 21.

43. Jon Gjerde and Carlton C. Qualey, *Norwegians in Minnesota* (St. Paul: Minnesota Historical Society Press, 2002), 2.

44. Carlton C. Qualey, *Norwegian Settlement in the United States* (New York: Arno Press, 1970), 9.

45. Byron J. Nordstrom, *Scandinavia Since 1500* (Minneapolis: University of Minnesota Press, 2001), 180.

46. Ingrid Semmingsen, *Norway to America: A History of the Migration* (Minneapolis: University of Minnesota Press, 1980), 120.

47. U.S. Census Bureau, Census 2000 Summary File 3, Matrices P1 and PCT18.

48. Qualey, *Norwegian Settlement in the United States*, 176–80.

49. Linda Christopherson, Norwegian Migration from Lier, Norway to Leer, Michigan (Mount Pleasant, Mich.: Unpublished student paper, 1966), 12–13, 19–20.

50. Qualey, *Norwegian Settlement in the United States*, 183–85.

51. Ibid., 183–86.

52. Arlow W. Andersen, *The Salt of the Earth: A History of Norwegian-Danish Methodism in America* (Nashville: Parthenon Press, 1962), 13.

53. E. Clifford Nelson, *Lutheranism in North America 1914–1970* (Minneapolis: Augsburg Publishing House, 1972), 3, 9.

54. Hjalmar Holand, "Norske Pionerer og Settlementer: Det Største Norske Settlement i Michigan," *Decorah Posten*, 5 and 12 December 1919.

55. Knut Gjerset, *Norwegian Sailors on the Great Lakes: A Chapter in the History of American Inland Transportation* (Northfield, Minn.: Norwegian-American Historical Association, 1928), 5, 16, 48.

56. Robert J. Henning, *Ships Gone Missing: The Great Lakes Storm of 1913* (Chicago: Contemporary Books, 1992), 1–5.

57. Gjerset, *Norwegian Sailors on the Great Lakes*, 117.

58. Ibid, 121.

59. Theodore J. Karamanski and Richard Zeitlin, *Narrative History of Isle Royale National Park* (Chicago: Loyola University of Chicago Mid-American Research Center, 1988), 164.

60. Dorothy Simonson, *The Diary of an Isle Royale School Teacher* (Houghton: Isle Royale Natural History Association, 1992).

61. Kenneth Bjork, *Saga in Steel and Concrete: Norwegian Engineers in America* (Northfield, Minn.: Norwegian-American Historical Association, 1947), 169–215.

For Further Reference

Ahlström, Göran. "The Edison of Sweden: c.e. Johansson and the 'Standards of Standard.'" *Lund Papers in Economic History* 71(2001): 1–14.

Allen, E. John. *From Skisport to Skiing: One Hundred Years of an American Sport, 1840–1940* (Amherst: University of Massachusetts Press, 1993), 47, 50–51.

Andersen, Arlow W. *The Salt of the Earth: A History of Norwegian-Danish Methodism in America.* Nashville: Parthenon Press, 1962.

Babcock, Kendric Charles. *The Scandinavian Element in the United States.* New York: Arno Press, 1969.

Beasley, Norman. *Knudsen: A Biography.* New York: Whittlesey House, 1947.

Bjork, Kenneth. *Saga in Steel and Concrete: Norwegian Engineers in America.* Northfield, Minn.: Norwegian-American Historical Association, 1947.

Blegen, Theodore C. *Norwegian Migration to America, 1825–1860.* Northfield, Minn.: Norwegian-American Historical Association, 1931.

Carlson, Bruce W. *History Along the Highways of America: Grayling.* Midland, Mich.: Pendell Publishing Company, 1973.

Christopherson, Linda. Norwegian Migration from Lier, Norway to Leer, Michigan. Mount Pleasant, Mich.: Unpublished student paper, 1966.

Dasef, John. *History of Montcalm County, Michigan, Its People, Industries and Institutions: With Biographical Sketches of Representative Citizens and*

Genealogical Records of Many of the Old Families. Indianapolis: B.F. Bowen and Co., 1919.

Eaton, Conan Bryant. "From Eyrarbakki to Muskegon: An Icelandic Saga," *Michigan History* 66, no. 3 (May/June, 1982): 13–15.

Englund, Eric. "Farmers." In *Swedes in America 1638–1938,* edited by Adolph B. Benson and Naboth Hedin. New Haven, Conn.: Yale University Press, 1938.

Fairbank, Henry W. *Report of the Commissioner of Immigration for the State of Michigan for the Years 1883 and 1884.* Lansing: W.S. George and Co., State Printers and Binders, 1885.

Feddersen, Christian T. *Scandinavians in Michigan: With Special Reference to Detroit and Environs.* Romeo, Mich.: self-published, 1968.

The First Hundred Years: An Introduction to the History of the Grayling Area. Grayling, Mich.: Grayling Area Centennial Committee, 1972.

Gjerde, Jon, and Carlton C. Qualey. *Norwegians in Minnesota.* St. Paul: Minnesota Historical Society Press, 2002.

Gjerset, Knut. *Norwegian Sailors on the Great Lakes: A Chapter in the History of American Inland Transportation.* Northfield, Minn.: Norwegian-American Historical Association, 1928.

Hale, Frederick. *Danes in North America.* Seattle: University of Washington Press, 1984.

Henning, Robert J. *Ships Gone Missing: The Great Lakes Storm of 1913.* Chicago: Contemporary Books, 1992.

"History Fans Push for More Markers for Western Sites," *Capital News Service, Michigan State University School of Journalism,* 2 April 2004.

Hoffenblad, Ludvig M. *Det Danske Søstersamfund i Amerika in Danske i Amerika* (Minneapolis: C. Rasmussen Publishing, 1908), 227–32.

Hoffsten, C. E. *The Swedish Element in America: A History of Swedish-American Achievements from 1638 to the Present Day.* 2nd ed. Vol. 4, *Swedish-American History in Lower Michigan.* Chicago: Swedish-American Biographical Society, 1934.

Holand, Hjalmar, "Norske Pionerer og Settlementer: Det Største Norske Settlement i Michigan," *Decorah Posten,* 5 and 12 December 1919.

Holmio, Armas K. E. *History of the Finns in Michigan.* Detroit: Wayne State University Press, 2001.

http://seaborg.nmu.edu/about/seaborg.html, accessed February 21, 2005.

http://www.skihall.com/history.htm, accessed December 2, 2004.

http://www.sofn.com/aboutus/History.html, accessed February 18, 2005.

http://www.vasaorder.com/aboutorg.htm, accessed January 31, 2005.

Janson, Florence F. *The Background of Swedish Immigration 1840–1930*. Chicago: University of Chicago Press, 1931.

Johnson, Amandus. "Colonists." In *Swedes in America 1638–1938*, edited by Adolph B. Benson and Naboth Hedin, 5–34. New Haven, Conn.: Yale University Press, 1938.

Johnson, Clarence H. "Origins, Population, Locations, Occupations and Activities of the Swedes in Detroit." Master's thesis, Wayne State University, 1940.

Karamanski, Theodore J., and Richard Zeitlin, *Narrative History of Isle Royale National Park*. Chicago: Loyola University of Chicago Mid-American Research Center, 1988.

Kinsey, Donald D. *Drill Cores: Folklore of Michigan's Upper Peninsula*. Unpublished ms.,Walter F. Gries Collection, Clarke Historical Library, Central Michigan University, 1959.

"Learn the Art of Living at Folk Schools: How Vacationists Have Mixed Knowledge With Sunshine at Meetings in Michigan," *Detroit News*, Metropolitan Section, 2 September 1928.

Leary, James P. *So Ole Says to Lena: Folk Humor of the Upper Midwest* (Madison: University of Wisconsin Press, 2001), 62.

Men of Progress of Michigan: Embracing Biographical Sketches of Representative Michigan Men with an Outline History of the State. Detroit: Evening New Association, 1900.

Mortensen, Enok. *The Danish Lutheran Church in America: The History and Heritage of the American Evangelical Lutheran Church*. Philadelphia: Board of Publication of the Lutheran Church in America, 1967.

Nelsen, Arthur. Unpublished memoirs of the Dane College, March 2004.

Nelson, E. Clifford. *Lutheranism in North America 1914-1970*. Minneapolis: Augsburg Publishing House, 1972.

Nielsen, George R. *The Danish Americans*. Boston: Twayne Publishers, 1981.

Nordal, Jóhannes. ed.., *Iceland 874–1974: Handbook Published by the Central Bank of Iceland on the Occasion of the Eleventh Centenary of the Settlement of Iceland*. Reykjavík: The Central Bank of Iceland, 1975.

Nordstrom, Byron J. Scandinavia Since 1500. Minneapolis: University of Minnesota Press, 2000.

Ojakangas, Beatrice A. *Scandinavian Cooking.* Minneapolis: University of Minnesota Press, 2003.

Olsson, Nils William. "The Swedish Settlement of Tustin, Michigan," *Swedish Pioneer Historical Quarterly* 12, no. 3 (July 1962): 109–13.

Qualey, Carlton C. *Norwegian Settlement in the United States.* New York: Arno Press, 1970.

Rasmussen, August. *Pioneer Life in the Big Dane Settlement.* Blair, Nebr.: Danish Lutheran Publishing House, 1904.

Rice, John G. "The Swedes." In *They Chose Minnesota: A Survey of the State's Ethnic Groups,* edited by June Drenning Holmquist, 248–54. St. Paul: Minnesota Historical Society Press, 1981.

Robertson, Augustine M. *Indians Sawmills and Danes: The Early History of the Flat River Area of Michigan.* Greenville, Mich.: Flat River Historical Society, 1971.

Romig, Walter. *Michigan Place Names: The History of the Founding and the Naming of More Than Five Thousand Past and Present Michigan Communities.* Grosse Point, Mich.: Walter Romig Publishing, 1973.

Semmingsen, Ingrid. *Norway to America: A History of the Migration.* Minneapolis: University of Minnesota Press, 1978.

Settlement Lutheran Church, Gowen, Michigan, *Centennial Anniversary 1873–1973.* Gowen, Mich.: Settlement Lutheran Church, 1973.

Silfversten, Carl J. *Finlandsvenskarna i Amerika: Deres Materiella och Andliga Strävanden.* Duluth: Self-published, 1931.

Simonson, Dorothy. *The Diary of an Isle Royale School Teacher.* Houghton: Isle Royale Natural History Association, 1992.

Smith, Franklin Campbell. *The Diocese of Western Michigan.* Grand Rapids: Diocesan Historical Commission, 1948.

Stefansson, Vilhjalmur. *Iceland: The First American Republic.* New York: Doubleday, Doran & Company, 1939.

Stengren, Alice. "A Danish Settlement in Grant, Michigan," Unpublished ms., Clarke Historical Library, Central Michigan University, 1970.

U.S. Census Bureau, Census 2000 Summary File 3, Matrices P1 and PCT18.

Viestad, Andreas. *Kitchen of Light: New Scandinavian Cooking with Andreas Viestad.* New York: Artisan Press, 2003.

Index